SpringerBriefs in Law

More information about this series at http://www.springer.com/series/10164

Robert Böttner · Jan Grinc

Bridging Clauses in European Constitutional Law

Legal Framework and Parliamentary Participation

Springer

Robert Böttner
German University of Administrative Sciences
Speyer
Germany

Jan Grinc
Faculty of Law
Charles University
Prague
Czech Republic

ISSN 2192-855X ISSN 2192-8568 (electronic)
SpringerBriefs in Law
ISBN 978-3-319-73340-1 ISBN 978-3-319-73341-8 (eBook)
https://doi.org/10.1007/978-3-319-73341-8

Library of Congress Control Number: 2017962540

Printed on acid-free paper

This Springer imprint is published by Springer Nature
The registered company is Springer International Publishing AG
The registered company address is: Gewerbestrasse 11, 6330 Cham, Switzerland

Preface

When the general bridging clauses were introduced into EU primary law by the Treaty of Lisbon, they initially sparked some debates in academia. Since then, however, it seems that the passerelle clauses have fallen into a state of hibernation—both in political practice and in academia. Only recently, they have reappeared on the political radar in Brussels, as both the Commission and the European Parliament have identified bridging clauses as one means to overcome the current paralysis of the European project. Nevertheless, there is still little research and a lot of questions remain unclear, especially with regard to the relationship between European and domestic law on parliamentary participation.

The present study tries to fill this gap. It is the outcome of an independent collaboration between the two authors, both of which have dealt with questions of parliamentary participation in EU affairs and treaty amendment procedures in their previous research.

We want to thank all colleagues from academia and the national Parliaments for their help and information on domestic procedures of parliamentary participation. All errors, however, remain in our responsibility. We hope that the study meets the interest of everyone involved with and interested in bridging clauses and that it may spark a debate and provide some guidance for future practice. We welcome any comments or questions at boettner@uni-speyer.de or grinc@prf.cuni.cz.

Speyer, Germany
Prague, Czech Republic
November 2017

Robert Böttner
Jan Grinc

Contents

Chapter 1
Introduction

Bridging clauses are no innovation of the Treaty of Lisbon, but certainly the introduction of a *general* bridging clause considerably broadens the scope of application. With a simple act of secondary law the voting procedures in the Treaties can be altered. While it seems that the passerelle clauses have fallen into a state of hibernation after their introduction, they can have considerable ramifications once they unfold their potential. At the same time, their non-use seems to go hand in hand with a certain lack of interest in legal research. The present study tries to fill this gap. The focus will be on the role of national Parliaments.

This introductory chapter will outline the framework in which the bridging clauses are located. For that purpose, it will start with a general outline of national parliamentary participation as foreseen by EU primary law (Sect. 1.1) and, specifically, in the procedures for the amendment of the Treaties (Sect. 1.2). In a second step, we will take a look at the coming into being of the bridging clauses in the current Treaty regime (Sect. 1.3).

The first main part of the study is dedicated to the substantial law of the general bridging clauses. We will first define the scope of application of the general passerelles (Sect. 2.1). This includes identifying when these clauses can be used (Sect. 2.3) and which written and unwritten exceptions exist (Sect. 2.2). Moreover, we will take a look at the relationship between the two general bridging clauses (Sect. 2.4) and the legal effects of the use of these clauses (Sect. 2.5).

The second part will then deal with the special bridging clauses that are scattered throughout the Treaties, most notably the sector-specific passerelle clauses (Sect. 3.1), the bridging clause for the area of enhanced cooperation (Sect. 3.2) as well as what we call the "semi-passerelle clauses" (Sect. 3.4). Of a special interest is the relationship between the bridging clause found in the area of the Common Foreign and Security Policy and the general bridging clauses (Sect. 3.3).

The third part of the study will tackle procedural issues. This requires first to take a look at the procedural requirements that are found in the provision itself. The important and most complex element is the participation of the national Parliaments (Sect. 4.1). The procedure itself begins with the initiative of the European Council

R. Böttner and J. Grinc, *Bridging Clauses in European Constitutional Law*,
SpringerBriefs in Law, https://doi.org/10.1007/978-3-319-73341-8_1

(Sect. 4.2), followed by the period for national parliamentary veto (Sect. 4.3), and the requirement of the European Parliament to give its consent (Sect. 4.4). Finally, the decision to activate a bridging clause is taken by the European Council. While European law does not make any further requirements, a number of national legal orders have installed more rigid safeguards and mandating systems for the national European Council representative (Sect. 4.5). We will also shortly discuss similar procedural issues related to special bridging clauses (Sect. 4.6).

Lastly, we will try and draw conclusions. This includes the question whether the bridging clauses will ever be used.

1.1 Parliamentary Participation in EU Affairs According to EU Primary Law

The last Treaty revision has profoundly changed the parliamentary dimension of the European Union's institutional setting. This is true for the European Parliament, which is now a true co-legislator, as the former co-decision procedure is now the default legislative procedure. It also acts as co-legislator in budgetary measures and has an important function in the election of the European Commission.

Furthermore, the Treaty of Lisbon has fundamentally altered the position of the national Parliaments within the Union's multilevel governance structure. The importance of the parliamentary dimension at Union level is spelled out by Article 10 TEU, which states in its paragraph 1, that the functioning of the Union shall be founded on representative democracy. As elaborated by paragraph 2, this means that citizens are directly represented at Union level in the European Parliament and that Member States are represented in the European Council by their Heads of State or Government and in the Council by their governments, themselves democratically accountable either to their national Parliaments, or to their citizens; the latter aspect reveals the national Parliaments' role in the indirect legitimation of Union power.[1] Based on this provision, a general postulate may be formulated that important binding decisions in the European Council and Council should not be taken *arbitrarily* by the Member State representatives, but rather in their continuous connection with the collective bodies representing the "institutional seat of popular sovereignty"[2] in the respective Member States. To ensure this is the task of both EU and national institutions, as documented precisely by the various EU and national legal arrangements pertaining to bridging clauses.

In addition, Article 12 TEU states that national Parliaments contribute actively to the good functioning of the Union. It lists the cases in which participation of national Parliaments as one of the constituent elements of Union action and in the

[1] See on this aspect also Blanke and Böttner (2015), p. 258 ff., with further references.

[2] von Beyme (1999), pp. 543–544.

further development of the Union is required. These cases are then specified in different parts of the Treaties.[3]

First, national Parliaments shall contribute through being informed by the institutions of the Union and having draft legislative acts of the Union forwarded to them in accordance with the Protocol on the role of national Parliaments in the European Union (Article 12(a) TEU). Besides the general obligation of the Union institutions, most notably the Commission, to inform national Parliaments in accordance with Article 12 TEU and Protocol No. 1, there are a number of other provisions that explicitly grant national Parliaments a right to be informed.[4] In this context, national Parliaments shall review draft legislation by seeing to it that the principle of subsidiarity is respected in accordance with the procedures provided for in the Protocol No. 2 on the application of the principles of subsidiarity and proportionality (Article 12(b) TEU).[5] While the information duties of the Commission or other EU institutions do not cover e.g. draft non-legislative acts,[6] in practice, the Commission transmits to the national Parliaments all the relevant documents it makes publicly available.[7]

Furthermore, the Parliaments of the Member States shall take part, within the framework of the area of freedom, security and justice, in the evaluation mechanisms for the implementation of the Union policies in that area, in accordance with Article 70 of the TFEU, and through being involved in the political monitoring of Europol and the evaluation of Eurojust's activities in accordance with Articles 88 and 85 of that Treaty (Article 12(c) TEU).

Moreover, national Parliaments are involved in the process of accession to the Union of new Member States (Article 12(e) TEU). They shall be notified of applications for accession to the Union, in accordance with Article 49 of the TEU. As that provision spells out, accession to the Union requires an agreement between the current Member States and the applicant State, which shall be submitted for ratification by all the contracting States in accordance with their respective constitutional requirements. This usually requires a parliamentary vote of consent.

Interestingly, the Treaties regard national Parliaments not only as individual players in the institutional and governance architecture of the Union. While rights granted by the Treaties can be exercised by national Parliaments only individually

---

[3]For an overview, see also the comments on Article 12 TEU by Calliess, in Calliess and Ruffert (2016), Hölscheidt, in Grabitz et al. (2017), Bieber, in von der Groeben et al. (2015).

[4]See the overview in Bieber, in von der Groeben et al. (2015), Article 12 EUV, para. 17.

[5]On the role of national Parliaments for the review of subsidiarity, see Kiiver (2011, 2012), Molsberger (2009), Schima (2013), see also the commentary on Protocol No. 2 in Blanke and Mangiameli (2013).

[6]Such as draft decisions under the special bridging clauses that do not include the parliamentary veto (see Chap. 3) or some of the decisions requiring approval by the Member States in accordance with their respective constitutional requirements listed in Sect. 1.2.5.

[7]The Commission uses the e-TrustEx platform (Electronic Trusted Exchange of Documents). Many of the documents are also published on IPEX, The platform for EU Interparliamentary Exchange established by EU Speakers' Conference, at www.ipex.eu.

(by the Parliaments as a whole or the component chambers), the Treaty provisions encourage coordination between the national Parliaments. They shall take part in inter-parliamentary cooperation with one another and with the European Parliament, in accordance with the Protocol on the role of national Parliaments in the European Union (Article 12(f) TEU). Article 10 of said Protocol deals with the role of COSAC (*Conférence des Organes Parlementaires Spécialisés dans les Affaires de l'Union des Parlements de l'Union Européenne*) as the most important forum of interparliamentary cooperation, but there are a number of others.[8]

1.2 Parliamentary Participation in Treaty Revision *Largo Sensu*

Lastly, national Parliaments shall take part in the revision procedures of the Treaties, in accordance with Article 48 of the TEU (Article 12(d) TEU) and with other special provisions of the Treaties.

1.2.1 General Remarks

Any amendment to or revision of the Treaties are changes of the international instruments constituting the international organisation "European Union". Generally, the ratification of international agreements (for the purpose of their entry into force) as well as any other subsequent change to those agreements requires the consent of the parliaments of the Contracting States, save as otherwise agreed in the treaty itself.[9]

For this reason, the Parliaments of the EU Member States are involved in the procedures for the amendment of the Treaties. Apart from the general Article 48 TEU, the Treaties contain a number of other provisions which lead or may lead to a material or a formal change in primary law. The Treaty makers regarded it necessary—in some, but not all of the cases—to include the national Parliaments in the procedures in order to compensate for the elimination of the normal ratification requirement.

At the same time, the level of participation of national Parliaments in these procedures stemming from European law is considered to be insufficient by some domestic constitutional systems. Therefore, some national legal orders have

---

[8]See Mayer (2012), p. 151 ff.; Calliess, in Calliess and Ruffert (2016), Article 12 EUV, para 80 ff.; Lupo, in Blanke and Mangiameli (2013), Protocol No. 1, para. 120 ff. (on Article 9); and Fasone, in Blanke and Mangiameli (2013), Protocol No. 1, para. 149 ff. (on Article 10); Dialer et al. (2015), pp. 309–340.

[9]Cf. Article 39 in combination with Part II (Articles 6 ff.) of the Vienna Convention on the Law of Treaties (1969), UN Treaty Series, vol. 1155, p. 331.

complemented the European law aspects of parliamentary involvement by national provisions or added such provisions to follow up on EU law clauses which do not provide for parliamentary involvement. These provisions mostly take the form of a "backup" procedure for the vote of the national (European) Council representative on the activation of the procedure in question, i.e. the vote of the national representative is dependent on a positive vote (authorisation) from his or her national Parliament.

The following section provides a brief overview of the various procedures in which the national Parliaments (and often also the European Parliament) participate.

The procedures for the amendment of the Treaties have been modified significantly by the Treaty of Lisbon. As mentioned, the central provision for Treaty revision is Article 48 of the TEU, which contains the default procedure for the amendment of the Treaties ("ordinary revision procedure") as well as two "simplified revision procedures".[10] It elaborates the procedures to be followed for the revision of the Treaties. Apart from any specific provisions (e.g. in the course of an accession, Article 49 TEU,[11] or a withdrawal, Article 50 TEU,[12]) primary law can only be modified by means of the amendment procedures carried out in accordance with Article 48 TEU.[13] This includes generally not only the Treaty on European Union and the Treaty on the Functioning of the European Union ("the Treaties" as mentioned by Article 1 TEU), but more comprehensively all primary law, including the Protocols (Article 51 TEU[14]), the Charter of Fundamental Rights (Article 6(1) TEU), the Euratom Treaty (by virtue of Article 106a(1) of said Treaty[15]) as well as the accession Treaties, unless these provide for specific amendment rules.[16]

1.2.2 *Ordinary Revision Procedure*

Paragraphs 2 through 5 of Article 48 TEU contain the rules on the ordinary revision procedure.[17] *De constitutione lata*, the general structure of this amendment procedure has been maintained, but the Treaty of Lisbon has brought about some

---

[10]See in more detail Peers (2012).

[11]Peers (2012), p. 47 ff.

[12]Peers (2012), p. 53 ff.

[13]European Court of Justice, Case 43/75, *Defrenne*, judgment of 8 April 1976, ECLI:EU:C:1976:56, para. 58.

[14]While the simplified revision procedures of Article 48 TEU shall not apply to amendments of Protocols, there are a number of provisions that provide for simplified revision of the Protocols; see Peers (2012), p. 66.

[15]Only the ordinary revision procedure of the TEU (Article 48, paragraphs 2–5) shall apply to the Euratom Treaty.

[16]On the latter, see Hillion (2004), p. 587; Ohler, in Grabitz et al. (2011), Artikel 48 EUV, para. 22.

[17]See on this also Böttner (2016), p. 500 ff.

profound changes to the existing Treaty revision procedure. Under the ordinary revision procedure, the directly elected European Parliament has been included among the actors who can initiate the procedure. Furthermore, before convening a conference of government representatives that decides on the proposed amendments, a convention is convened by the European Council. The participants to this convention include not only government representatives, but also representatives of the national Parliaments, the European Parliament and the Commission, i.e. representatives from the executive and the legislative branch at the national and the European level.[18] This inclusion of other actors enhances transparency and makes Treaty revisions less of a diplomatic negotiation between governments,[19] but rather a truly supranational procedure.[20] Furthermore, fundamental change to the Treaties can only be made through this convention method, as it confers a higher degree of democratic legitimacy.[21] One element, however, remains and is reminiscent of the Union's origin in public international law and of its being a treaty-based creation among sovereign states: before entering into force, every amendment to the Treaties has to be ratified by all Member States in accordance with their national procedures. With a growing number of Member States, this may turn out to be an extremely relevant obstacle.[22]

The ordinary revision procedure also allows the European Council to decide by a simple majority, after obtaining the consent of the European Parliament, not to convene a Convention should this not be justified by the extent of the proposed amendments. In this case, the European Council shall define the terms of reference for a conference of representatives of the governments of the Member States. Since the entry into force of the Lisbon Treaty, there have been two amendments made through the ordinary revision procedure, both without convening the Convention.[23]

1.2.3 Simplified Revision Procedure

Apart from the procedural simplifications in the ordinary revision procedure, the most innovative change is the introduction of simplified revision procedures. By

[18]Jimena Quesada (2012), p. 326.

[19]Busia (2010), p. 405.

[20]Cf. Ohler, in Grabitz et al. (2011), Artikel 48 EUV, para. 29.

[21]German Federal Constitutional Court, 2 BvR 2728/13 et al., *Treaty of Lisbon*, judgment of 30 June 2009, ECLI:DE:BVerfG:2009:es20090630.2bve000208, para. 309; Terhechte (2008), p. 169; Granat (2016), p. 73.

[22]Busia (2010), p. 404.

[23]Namely, an amendment to the Protocol on transitional provisions (O.J. EU 2010 C 263/1) and the addition of the Protocol on the concerns of the Irish people (O.J. EU 2013 L 60/131).

means of these procedures, amendments to the Treaties are possible without the full range of formalities of the previous standard revision procedure.[24]

The first simplified procedure (paragraph 6 of Article 48 TEU) authorises the European Council, on a proposal from the government of any Member State, the European Parliament or the Commission, to adopt a unanimous decision that amends the Treaties without an Intergovernmental Conference. That decision shall not enter into force until it is approved by the Member States in accordance with their respective constitutional requirements. The procedure may be used for revising all or part of the provisions of Part Three of the Treaty on the Functioning of the European Union relating to the internal policies and action of the Union as long as this does not increase the competences conferred on the Union in the Treaties. The procedure has been used for amending Article 136 of the TFEU by adding a paragraph 3 as the European law basis for the establishment of the European Stability Mechanism.[25]

The mode of parliamentary participation depends on the interpretation of the notion of "approval by the Member States in accordance with their respective constitutional requirements". Since the provision is a part of a *Treaty revision* procedure, it may be interpreted as referring simply to national procedures for ratification of international treaties or to the adoption of international obligations in a broader sense. Some Member States expressly refer to their rules for approval of international treaties,[26] others have established special procedures which are mostly modelled after their treaty ratification procedures.[27] Member States without a special procedure treated the decision of the European Council to amend Article 136 TFEU as an international agreement and applied the relevant general procedure for ratification.[28] There are also Member States where the very consent of the

[24]An overview over the different possibilities to amend the Treaties besides the ordinary procedure is found in Piris (2010), p. 361 ff.

[25]Decision 2011/199/EU, O.J. EU 2011 L 91/1; see on this Böttner (2016), p. 502; see in detail also Peers (2012), p. 33 ff.

[26]**Austria**: Article 23i(4) of the Constitution; **Czech Republic**: Section 109l of the Rules of Procedure of the Chamber of Deputies and Section 119o of the Standing Rules of the Senate.

[27]Usually ratification through an act of parliament is required. **Germany**: Section 2 of the Act on the Exercise by the Bundestag and by the Bundesrat of their Responsibility for Integration in Matters concerning the European Union referring to Article 23(1) of the Basic Law; **Ireland**: the decision amending Article 136 TFEU has been expressly added by the European Communities (Amendment) Act 2012 to the list of "treaties governing the EU" requiring ratification through a legislative act of parliament; **Italy**: Article 11 of the Law No. 234/2012 of 24 December 2012 on general rules on Italy's participation in formation and implementation of EU legislation and policies; **Malta**: Article 2(2) of the European Union Act; **United Kingdom**: Sections. 3–5 of theEuropean Union Act 2011.

[28]Belgium, Bulgaria, Cyprus, Estonia, Finland, France, Greece, Hungary, Latvia, Lithuania, Luxembourg, Poland, Portugal, Romania, Slovakia, Slovenia, Spain, Sweden. See in detail for individual Member States the database *Constitutional Change through Euro Crisis Law. A Multi-level Legal Analysis.* EUI, 2015 [2017-10-15]. http://eurocrisislaw.eui.eu/topic/tfeu/.

national European Council representative with the adoption of the decision according to Article 48(6) TEU is subject to special parliamentary control.[29]

1.2.4 General Bridging Clauses as Another Simplified Revision Procedure

By means of the second simplified revision procedure of Article 48 TEU (paragraph 7), the so called general bridging clauses or "passerelles", the European Council may decide to shift from a special legislative procedure provided for in the Treaties to the ordinary legislative procedure or from a required unanimity in the Council to qualified majority voting. This shall make it possible—once political agreement has been reached among the Member States—to shift from intergovernmental to supranational decision-making and voting procedures by means of an act of secondary law and not through the cumbersome ordinary revision procedure. In order to provide for a sufficient level of democratic legitimation for this form of flexible Treaty revision, national Parliaments are involved, but not, however, in the form of a positive consent, instead by means of a veto right (see Sect. 4.3).

1.2.5 Decisions Requiring the Approval by the Member States in Accordance with Their Respective Constitutional Requirements

Among the other relevant provisions allowing to amend the Treaties without activating the revision procedure of Article 48 TEU is first and foremost the group of decisions that enter into force following an "approval by the Member States in accordance with their respective constitutional requirements", i.e. with the same reservation as in Article 48(6) TEU. These cases are:

- the abovementioned amendment by accession in accordance with Article 49 TEU;
- the establishment of a common defence: In accordance with Article 42(2) of the TEU, the Union's common security and defence policy shall include the progressive framing of a common Union defence policy. This will lead to a common defence, when the European Council, acting unanimously, so decides.

[29]**Germany**: special procedure of reconciliation of opinions between the Federal Government and the Bundestag before a decision by the European Council on Treaty amendment is adpoted (Section 9 of the Act on Cooperation between the Federal Government and the German Bundestag in Matters Concerning the European Union); **Czech Republic**: previous consent of both chambers of Parliament according to Section 109i(b) of the Rules of Procedure of the Chamber of Deputies and Section 119k(b) of the Standing Rules of the Senate.

It shall in that case recommend to the Member States the adoption of such a decision in accordance with their respective constitutional requirements.[30]

- the extension of the rights of the Union citizens: As Article 25 of the TFEU provides, the Commission shall regularly report to the European Parliament, to the Council and to the Economic and Social Committee on the status and the development of the Union citizens' rights. On the basis of this report, the Council, acting unanimously in accordance with a special legislative procedure and after obtaining the consent of the European Parliament, may adopt provisions to strengthen or to add to the rights listed in Article 20(2) TFEU. These provisions shall enter into force after their approval by the Member States in accordance with their respective constitutional requirements.
- the Union's accession to the European Convention for the Protection of Human Rights and Fundamental Freedoms (ECHR): Article 6(2) of the TEU authorises, but also contains the obligation for the Union to accede to the ECHR. As an international agreement the accession agreement is subject to the procedure of Article 218 of the TFEU. As a rule, the decision concluding the international agreement is taken by the Council by qualified majority after consulting or after obtaining the consent of the European Parliament. As an exception, however, Article 218(8) of the TFEU provides that the Council shall act unanimously for the agreement on accession of the Union to the ECHR and the decision concluding this agreement shall enter into force after it has been approved by the Member States in accordance with their respective constitutional requirements.
- the adoption of a uniform electoral procedure for elections to the European Parliament: In accordance with Article 223(1) TFEU, the European Parliament shall draw up a proposal to lay down the provisions necessary for the election of its Members by direct universal suffrage in accordance with a uniform procedure in all Member States or in accordance with principles common to all Member States. The Council, acting unanimously in accordance with a special legislative procedure and after obtaining the consent of the European Parliament, which shall act by a majority of its component Members, shall lay down the necessary provisions. These provisions shall enter into force following their approval by the Member States in accordance with their respective constitutional requirements.
- the establishment of intellectual property rights litigation: on the basis of Article 262 of the TFEU, the Council, acting unanimously in accordance with a special legislative procedure and after consulting the European Parliament, may adopt provisions to confer jurisdiction on the Court of Justice of the European Union in disputes relating to the application of acts adopted on the basis of the Treaties which create European intellectual property rights. These provisions shall enter

[30]For reasons unclear, Article 42(2) TEU differs in its wording from the other cases listed here. The "recommendation" of the European Council should not be interpreted as making the national adoption of the decision facultative. It rather seems that unlike the other cases, the decision on common defence could have the form of an international treaty concluded in the European Council.

into force after their approval by the Member States in accordance with their respective constitutional requirements.

- the Union's own resources decision: As provided in Article 311 of the TFEU, the Union shall provide itself with the means necessary to attain its objectives and carry through its policies. To this end, the Council, acting in accordance with a special legislative procedure, shall unanimously and after consulting the European Parliament adopt a decision laying down the provisions relating to the system of own resources of the Union. In this context it may establish new categories of own resources or abolish an existing category. That decision shall not enter into force until it is approved by the Member States in accordance with their respective constitutional requirements.

In general, the interpretation of these provisions can be the same as that of Article 48(6) TEU, i.e. national treaty ratification rules apply, unless determined otherwise. Given the variety of the above mentioned cases—some of which would constitute amendments to primary law (accession of a new member, extension of the citizens' rights, arguably also the common defence), while others would not necessarily have to amount to changes in primary law at all despite their political importance (decision on own resources)—a differentiated approach in national law cannot be ruled out.

Most Member States have left the question of approval in accordance with the constitutional requirements open to the interpretation by the constitutional bodies. This may mean the use of standard procedures for the adoption of international obligations or even no special approval at all.[31] Some Member States refer to the procedure for ratification of international treaties,[32] or to the adoption of a law (which may also be the ordinary means for giving effect to an international agreement in the national legal order).[33] In case of Article 42(2) TEU, some

[31]The Member State would then "approve" the decision simply by effecting the necessary changes to national law resulting from the EU act. It may be argued that in the discussed cases—as opposed to classic implementation of EU acts whose entry into force is not subject to "approval of the Member States"—the Member State would not be under an *obligation* to make the changes to national law. The adoption of national legal enactments would be the means of approval of the decision and therefore a matter of political choice of the Member State. Such a conduct would however have to respect the principle of sincere cooperation (Article 4(3) TEU).

[32]**Austria**: Article 23i(4) of the Constitution; **Italy**: Article 11(3) of the Law No. 234/2012 of 24 December 2012 on general rules on Italy's participation in formation and implementation of EU legislation and policies; **Poland**: Article 23 of the Act of 8 October 2010 on the cooperation of the Council of Ministers with the Sejm and the Senate in matters relating to the Republic of Poland's membership of the European Union.

[33]**Austria**: Article 23i(3) of the Constitution (in case of Article 311 TFEU); **Germany**: Section 3 of the Act on the Exercise by the Bundestag and by the Bundesrat of their Responsibility for Integration in Matters concerning the European Union; **Italy**: Article 11(6) of the Law No. 234/2012 of 24 December 2012 on general rules on Italy's participation in formation and implementation of EU legislation and policies (in case of Article 311 TFEU); **Lithuania**: § 180[26] of the Statute of the Seimas; **United Kingdom**: Section 7 of the European Union Act 2011 (for the establishment of common defence, Section 7 of the Act requires an approval by a referendum).

Member States allow their representatives in the European Council to vote for establishing the common defence only after obtaining the consent of the national Parliament.[34]

1.2.6 Special Bridging Clauses

While the parliamentary participation with respect to the cases mentioned above in Sect. 1.2.5 is similar in its construction to the simplified Treaty revision procedure of Article 48(6) TEU, there is also one special bridging clause that follows the pattern of the general bridging clauses of Article 48(7) TEU including the national parliamentary veto. This is found in the second and third subparagraph of Article 81(3) TFEU, which allows the passing to ordinary legislative procedure in certain aspects of family law with cross-border implications.

Then there are other special bridging clauses do not provide for a veto of national Parliaments:

- passing to qualified majority voting in the Council in the Common Foreign and Security Policy according to Article 31(3) TEU;
- passing to ordinary legislative procedure in certain areas of social policy according to Article 153(2)(4) TFEU;
- passing to ordinary legislative procedure in certain areas of environmental policy according to Article 192(2) TFEU;
- passing to qualified majority voting in the Council when adopting the multi-annual financial framework according to Article 312(2) TFEU;
- passing to qualified majority voting in the Council and/or to ordinary legislative procedure within the framework of enhanced cooperation according to Article 333 TFEU.

The special bridging clauses are discussed in detail in Chap. 3. The national parliamentary procedures are mentioned in Sect. 4.6.

[34]**Germany**: Section 3(3) of the Act on the Exercise by the Bundestag and by the Bundesrat of their Responsibility for Integration in Matters concerning the European Union; **Ireland**: Article 29 (9) of the Constitution, which prohibits Ireland from adopting the decision taken by the European Council to establish a common defence pursuant to Article 42(2) TEU where that common defence would include Ireland; **Italy**: Article 11(2) of the Law No. 234/2012 of 24 December 2012 on general rules on Italy's participation in formation and implementation of EU legislation and policies; **Poland**: Article 14 of the Act of 8 October 2010 on the cooperation of the Council of Ministers with the Sejm and the Senate in matters relating to the Republic of Poland's membership of the European Union.

1.2.7 Other Treaty-Amending Provisions

There are further clauses that provide for possible amendment of the primary law without even implicitly reserving a role for the national Parliaments:

- the extension of the list of serious crime with a cross-border dimension, Article 83(1)(3) TFEU[35];
- the extension of the powers of the European Public Prosecutor's Office (EPPO), Article 86(4) TFEU.[36]

The list of Treaty provisions on the boundary of Treaty amendment which have elicited in the national law a specific regulation of parliamentary participation is not exhaustive. Most notably, the unanimous adoption by the Council of a legal act on the basis of the flexibility clause of Article 352 TFEU, i.e. without there being a legal basis for such an action in the Treaties, may be subject to parliamentary consent.[37] In some Member States, national law also grants the parliament the right

[35]Again, in some Member States the approval of this act on behalf of the Member State is subject to parliamentary control: **Germany**: prior consent in the form of a law according to Section 7 of the Act on the Exercise by the Bundestag and by the Bundesrat of their Responsibility for Integration in Matters concerning the European Union; **Ireland**: prior approval by both chambers of the Parliament according to Article 29(8) of the Constitution; **Poland**: the Government shall seek the opinion of the Diet, but does not have to follow it; the Government only has to explain its reasons for not taking the Diet's opinion into consideration (see Articles 12 and 13 of the Act of 8 October 2010 on the cooperation of the Council of Ministers with the Sejm and the Senate in matters relating to the Republic of Poland's membership of the European Union); **United Kingdom**: prior consent by both chambers according to Section 9 of the European Union Act 2011.

[36]**Germany**, **Ireland** and **Poland** as in the previous footnote. The regulation establishing EPPO has recently been adopted by means of enhanced cooperation: Council Regulation (EU) 2017/1939 of 12 October 2017 implementing enhanced cooperation on the establishment of the European Public Prosecutor's Office ('the EPPO'), O.J. EU 2017 L 283/1. In its 2018 work programme, the Commission announced that it will propose the activation of Article 86(4) TFEU in order to extend the powers of the EPPO to prosecution of terrorism. Communication from the Commission to the European Parliament, the Council, the European Economic and Social Committee and the Committee of the Regions: Commission Work Programme 2018—An agenda for a more united, stronger and more democratic Europe, COM(2017) 650 of 24 October 2017 at p. 12.

[37]**Czech Republic**: prior consent of both chambers unless the proposal based on the flexibility clause is necessary for the operation of the common market (see Section 109i(f) of the Rules of Procedure of the Chamber of Deputies, Section 119k(d) of the Standing Rules of the Senate); **Germany**: prior consent in the form of a law according to Section 8 of the Act on the Exercise by the Bundestag and by the Bundesrat of their Responsibility for Integration in Matters concerning the European Union; **United Kingdom**: generally, prior consent by both chambers according to Section 8 of the European Union Act 2011. It is worth mentioning that the strict German regulation has led to substantial delays in adoption of measures based on Article 352 TFEU and in some cases the Commission withdrew its proposal that became outdated. See e.g. German Bundestag Print No. 18/2953 related to the Proposal for a Council Decision on a Tripartite Social Summit for Growth and Employment (COM(2013) 740) and the withdrawn Proposal for a Council Decision amending Decision (2008/203/EC) of 28 February 2008 implementing Regulation

to oblige the national Council representative to make use of the emergency brake mechanism in Article 82(3)(1) sentence 1 or Article 83(3)(1) sentence 1 of the TFEU and of Article 31(2) TEU.[38] Certainly the most complex regulation of parliamentary participation based on the requirement of a previous parliamentary consent with the use of various provisions of the Treaties can be found in the United Kingdom (the 2011 European Union Act).

Finally, it needs to be stressed that the lack of specific procedures for parliamentary participation in the above mentioned cases in many Member States may simply be the result of subsumption of the relevant Treaty procedures under the general rules for parliamentary review and approval of negotiating mandates of national Council and European Council members, which are applicable to any EU matter. This so-called mandating system has been famously pioneered in Denmark.[39]

1.3 The Evolution of the General Bridging Clauses

Bridging clauses as such are not an invention of the Constitutional Convention or the Treaty makers of Lisbon. The EC Treaty already contained a few sector specific *passerelle* clause, e.g. the one in Article 67(2), second indent. According to that provision, the Council, acting unanimously after consulting the European Parliament, could take a decision with a view to providing for all or parts of the areas covered by the title on visa, asylum, migration and other policies related to free movement of persons (Articles 61 ff. of the EC Treaty) to be governed by the codecision procedure.[40] The "revolution" of the European Constitution was the introduction of *general* bridging clauses.

The introduction of a general bridging clause was not even hinted at in the Laeken Declaration.[41] At the European Convention, it was allegedly only discussed in the final weeks. Apparently, it came into being by scaling down a proposal to introduce an autonomous "European ratification" procedure, where the European Parliament and a qualified majority in the Council could amend the Constitution

(EC) No 168/2007 as regards the adoption of a Multi-annual Framework for the European Union Agency for Fundamental Rights for 2007–2012 (COM(2010) 708).

[38]Obligation of the government to activate the "brake clause" if requested by parliament in **Italy** according to Article 12 of the Law No. 234/2012 of 24 December 2012 on general rules on Italy's participation in formation and implementation of EU legislation and policies) and in **Germany** (for the TFEU cases only) according to Section 9 of the Act on the Exercise by the Bundestag and by the Bundesrat of their Responsibility for Integration in Matters concerning the European Union.

[39]Cf. e.g. Mayer (2012), pp. 177–211; Christensen (2015).

[40]See Council Decision 2004/927/EC of 22 December 2004 providing for certain areas covered by Title IV of Part Three of the Treaty establishing the European Community to be governed by the procedure laid down in Article 251 of that Treaty, O.J. EU 2004 L 396/45.

[41]Laeken Declaration on the Future of the European Union, European Council Conclusions, 14–15 December 2001, SN 300/01.

without subsequent national ratification, if the amendment did not affect the distribution of competences between the Union and the Member States.[42]

The European Convention's draft Treaty establishing a Constitution for Europe provided in its Article I-24(4) the following two procedures:

- Where the Constitution provides in Part III for European laws and framework laws to be adopted by the Council of Ministers according to a special legislative procedure, the European Council can adopt, on its own initiative and by unanimity, after a period of consideration of at least six months, a decision allowing for the adoption of such European laws or framework laws according to the ordinary legislative procedure. The European Council shall act after consulting the European Parliament and informing the national Parliaments.
- Where the Constitution provides in Part III for the Council of Ministers to act unanimously in a given area, the European Council can adopt, on its own initiative and by unanimity, a European decision allowing the Council of Ministers to act by qualified majority in that area. Any initiative taken by the European Council under this subparagraph shall be sent to national Parliaments no less than four months before any decision is taken on it.

We can see that no veto power for national Parliaments or the European Parliament was initially proposed, but there is already the mandatory "period of consideration" during which the European Parliament would have been consulted in case of switching from special to ordinary legislative procedure and during which there would also have been enough time for the national Parliaments to discuss the proposal with their governments.

The late introduction of the bridging clause to the Convention deliberations together with its political sensitivity may have been the cause of significant changes of the provision at the 2003–2004 Intergovernmental Conference. The various "evolutive" provisions that found their way into the Treaty establishing a Constitution for Europe (e.g. the simplified revision procedure which took up the idea of "European ratification") also required a coherent regulation of the procedural aspects, including the participation of national Parliaments and the European Parliament.

At the beginning of the Intergovernmental Conference, the Commission expressed its fear of "total paralysis of the Union", should the requirement of unanimous agreement of the Member States on any revision of primary law be maintained, and called for a competence of the European Council "to make amendments to Part III of the Constitution, deciding by a 5/6 majority of its members, following approval by the European Parliament and a favourable opinion from the Commission; unanimity would remain a requirement in cases where the proposed amendment would alter the Union's competences or the balance between

---

[42]Kiljunen (2004), pp. 145–147. This author suggests that the initative came from the Belgian Vice-President of the Convention *Jean-Luc Dehaene*, who "considered that the greatest weakness of the draft Constitution was that amendments to it would continue to require national ratification and unanimity" and promoted the "European ratification" procedure described above.

the institutions. These revisions would not be subject to ratification, but the national Parliaments should be involved ahead of any decision taken by the European Council, by way of the role they would play in a Convention and by dint of their watchdog role vis-à-vis government action."[43]

Later on, a joint declaration of parliamentary members of the European Convention addressed to the European Council stated that "[t]he passerelle provisions, triggered by a unanimous decision of the European Council … must be maintained as a key element of the evolutive nature of the Constitution"[44] without making any reference to parliamentary control over these decisions.

It seems that the direct participation of national Parliaments in the bridging clause mechanism was an idea conceived by the Member States. At some point in the negotiations, a collective veto power of an unspecified number of national Parliaments was apparently considered. A note from the presidency to the delegations of 25 November 2003 stated that "[i]n the light of the discussions on simplified procedures for revising the Constitutional Treaty, the Presidency proposes to address the issue in two ways: a) as to the decision to move from unanimity to qualified majority, or from a special legislative procedure to the ordinary legislative procedure (general bridging clause), it is proposed that the text be amended to include a provision whereby that decision would not come into effect if [X] national parliaments raise an objection ("nihil obstat" procedure)".[45]

Eventually, this evolved into an individual veto power of any national Parliament. The inclusion of European Parliament's consent in the procedure may have been a by-product of adding the national Parliaments' veto (an endeavour to strike a balance between the parliaments), or a partial adoption of the idea of "European ratification" as supported by the Commission in its communication to the Intergovernmental Conference. The final wording of the Treaty establishing a Constitution for Europe (Article IV-444) is materially the same as the current general bridging clauses introduced by the Lisbon Treaty.

---

[43]Communication from the Commission, A Constitution for the Union. Opinion of the Commission, pursuant to Article 48 of the Treaty on European Union, on the Conference of representatives of the Member States' governments convened to revise the Treaties, COM(2003) 548 final, p. 7.

[44]Joint Declaration addressed to the European Council by Parliamentary members of the European Convention, reunited in Brussels on Friday 5 December 2003. URL: http://www.cvce.eu/obj/declaration_by_parliamentary_members_of_the_european_convention_brussels_5_december_2003-en-c463343d-24e4-4116-9a37-7371306fdd78.html.

[45]Note from the Presidency to Delegations, CIG52/1/03 REV1(en)-PRESID 10. Brussels: Conference of the representatives of the governments of the Member States, 25.11.2003. 14 p. "IGC 2003-Naples Ministerial Conclave: Presidency proposal", p. 8. http://www.cvce.eu/obj/document_from_the_2003_igc_naples_ministerial_conclave_25_november_2003-en-6169c7c2-6896-4587-a107-ea6a396ab6b5.html. The draft article can be found in "IGC 2003—Naples Ministerial Conclave: Presidency proposal" from 25. November 2003, CIG/50/03 ADD 1. http://register.consilium.europa.eu/doc/srv?l=EN&t=PDF&f=CG+52+2003+ADD+1.

References

Blanke H-J, Böttner R (2015) The democratic deficit in the economic governance of the European Union. In Blanke H-J, Cruz Villalón P, Klein T, Ziller J (eds) Common European Legal Thinking. Essays in Honour of Albrecht Weber. Springer, Heidelberg, pp 243–286

Blanke H-J, Mangiameli S (eds) (2013) The Treaty on European Union—A commentary. Springer, Heidelberg

Böttner R (2016) The treaty amendment procedures and the relationship between Article 31(3) TEU and the general bridging clause of Article 48(7) TEU. Eur Const Law Rev 499–521

Busia G (2010) Revisione del Trattato, ammissione di nuovi Stati e recess dall'Unione. In: Bassanini F, Tiberi G (eds) Le nuove istituzioni europee. il Mulino, Bologna. pp 401–414

Calliess C, Ruffert M (eds) (2016) EUV/AEUV, 5th edn. C.H.Beck, Munich

Christensen MB (2015) The Danish Folketing and EU Affairs: is the Danish model of parliamentary scrutiny still best practice? In: Hefftler C, Neuhold C, Rozenberg O, Smith J (eds) The Palgrave handbook of national parliaments and the European Union. Palgrave, Basingstoke, pp 275–289

Dialer D, Maurer A, Richter M (2015) Handbuch zum Europäischen Parlament. Nomos, Baden-Baden

Grabitz E, Hilf M, Nettesheim M (eds) (2009 ff.) Das Recht der Europäischen Union: EUV/ AEUV. Loose leaf. C.H.Beck, Munich

Granat K (2016) Interparliamentary cooperation and the simplified revision procedures. In: Lupo N, Fasone C (eds) Interparliamentary cooperation in the composite European constitution. Hart, Oxord, pp 73–90

Hillion C (2004) The European Union is dead. Long live the European Union...A Commentary on the Accession Treaty 2003. Eur Law Rev 583–612

Jimena Quesada, J. (2012). The revision procedures of the treaty. In Blanke H-J, Mangiameli (eds) The European Union after Lisbon. Springer, Heidelberg, pp 323–342

Kiiver P (2011) The early-warning system for the principle of subsidiarity: the national parliament as a conseil d'etat for Europe. Eur Law Rev 98–108

Kiiver P (2012) The early warning system for the principle of subsidiarity. Routledge, London

Kiljunen K (2004) The European Constitution in the making. Centre for European Policy Studies, Brussels

Mayer M (2012) Die Europafunktion der nationalen Parlamente in der Europäischen Union. Mohr Siebeck, Tübingen

Molsberger P (2009) Das Subsidiaritätsprinzip im Prozess europäischer Konstitutionalisierung. Duncker & Humblot, Berlin

Peers S (2012) The future of EU treaty amendments. Yearb Eur Law 17–111

Piris J-C (2010) The Lisbon treaty: a legal and political analysis. Cambridge University Press, Cambridge

Schima B (2013) Die Subsidiaritätskontrolle durch die nationalen Parlamente nach dem Vertrag von Lissabon – einige praktische Bemerkungen aus der Sicht der Europäischen Kommission. Zeitschrift für öffentliches Recht 369–387

Terhechte JP (2008) Der Vertrag von Lissabon: Grundlegende Verfassungsurkunde der europäischen Rechtsgemeinschaft oder technischer Änderungsvertrag?. Europarecht 143–189

von Beyme K (1999) Die parlamentarische Demokratie: Entstehung und Funktionsweise 1789–1999, 3rd edn. Westdeutscher Verlag, Opladen/Wiesbaden

von der Groeben H, Schwarze J, Hatje A (eds) (2015) Europäisches Unionsrecht, 7th edn. Nomos, Baden-Baden

Chapter 2
The General Bridging Clauses of Article 48(7) TEU

The general *passerelles* are found in the Union's constitution among the provisions on Treaty amendments in Article 48(7) TEU. The final wording in the Treaty reads:

> Where the Treaty on the Functioning of the European Union or Title V of this Treaty provides for the Council to act by unanimity in a given area or case, the European Council may adopt a decision authorising the Council to act by a qualified majority in that area or in that case. This subparagraph shall not apply to decisions with military implications or those in the area of defence.
>
> Where the Treaty on the Functioning of the European Union provides for legislative acts to be adopted by the Council in accordance with a special legislative procedure, the European Council may adopt a decision allowing for the adoption of such acts in accordance with the ordinary legislative procedure.
>
> Any initiative taken by the European Council on the basis of the first or the second subparagraph shall be notified to the national Parliaments. If a national Parliament makes known its opposition within six months of the date of such notification, the decision referred to in the first or the second subparagraph shall not be adopted. In the absence of opposition, the European Council may adopt the decision.
>
> For the adoption of the decisions referred to in the first and second subparagraphs, the European Council shall act by unanimity after obtaining the consent of the European Parliament, which shall be given by a majority of its component members.

The following section will deal with these general bridging clauses. To this end, we will first take a look at the scope of application (Sects. 2.1 and 2.3) as well as at the exceptions (Sect. 2.2) of the general bridging clauses and their relationship towards one another (Sect. 2.4), followed by an inquiry into the legal effects (Sect. 2.5).

2.1 Scope of Application

Article 48(7) TEU contains the two general bridging clauses. On the basis of Article 48(7)(1) TEU the European Council, after obtaining the consent of the European Parliament, may unanimously adopt a decision authorising the Council to act by a qualified majority where the TFEU or Title V of the TEU provide for the Council to

R. Böttner and J. Grinc, *Bridging Clauses in European Constitutional Law*, SpringerBriefs in Law, https://doi.org/10.1007/978-3-319-73341-8_2

act by unanimity in a given area or case. This shall not apply to decisions with military implications or those in the area of defence. Likewise, under Article 48(7)(2) TEU, where the TFEU[1] provides for legislative acts to be adopted by the Council in accordance with a special legislative procedure, the European Council, after obtaining the consent of the European Parliament, may adopt a decision allowing for the adoption of such acts in accordance with the ordinary legislative procedure laid down in Articles 289(1), 294 TFEU.

There is an important limitation to the scope of application of the general bridging clauses. They do not cover *all* cases in which the Treaties provide for the adoption of an act in accordance with a special legislative procedure or decision making by special voting requirements apart from the default voting rules (European Parliament: simple majority, Article 231(1) TFEU; Council: qualified majority, Article 16(3) TEU). Instead, they apply only in cases where *the Council* acts by unanimity or where *the Council* adopts a legislative act. This means that the bridging clauses cannot be used to change voting requirements in the European Parliament (absolute majority to relative majority) nor can they be used in cases where a legislative act is adopted in accordance with a special legislative procedure, but not by the Council. This is the case for Article 223(2) TFEU concerning the conditions governing the performance of the duties of the Members of the European Parliament, Article 226(3) TFEU concerning the committee of inquiry, and Article 228(4) TFEU on the European Ombudsman. In those cases, relating to classical parliamentary rights, it is the European Parliament and not the Council who adopts the legislative act. Furthermore, the bridging clauses do not apply to the adoption of the annual budget in accordance with Article 314 TFEU. While the adoption of the annual budget shall be subject to a special legislative procedure, it cannot be said that it is the Council who will adopt the final act. Instead, the act is adopted jointly by the European Parliament and the Council, acting in their capacity as co-legislators in budgetary matters (Article 14(1) and Article 16(1) TEU).

With the exception of the admission of new Member States in accordance with Article 49(1) TEU the general bridging clauses cover all cases in which the Treaties provide for Council decision-making by unanimity or the adoption of legislative acts by the Council in accordance with a special legislative procedure. Apart from this, there are a few cases in which the Protocols, which are annexed to the Treaties, contain provisions that provide for the adoption of legal acts by the Council by unanimity or a special legislative procedure. The question thus arises whether the bridging clauses can be applied to these provisions as well.

According to the wording of Article 48(7) TEU, the general bridging clauses cover the TFEU and Title V of the TEU. As Article 51 TEU provides, the Protocols and Annexes to the Treaties shall form an integral part thereof. This means that,

[1] The second subparagraph does not apply to the Common Foreign and Security Policy anyway, which is covered by the TEU, as the adoption of legislative acts is excluded in this policy area (Article 24(1)(2), sentence 3, and Article 31(1)(1), sentence 2, of the TEU) and hence no legislative procedure applies (cf. Article 289(3) TFEU).

different from the Charter of Fundamental Rights of the European Union, which is a separate legal document which has the same legal (primary law) value as the Treaties (Article 6(1)(1) TEU), the Protocols are primary law *and* a constituent element of the Treaties themselves.[2] Furthermore, the Protocols supplement provisions of the Treaties. Thus, the subject matters and policy areas in the Protocols that contain voting or legislative procedures are comparable to those in the Treaties. Hence, according to the *telos* of the bridging clauses of gradually abolishing the special voting and legislative procedures and transpose them into the default voting and legislative procedures, it is reasonable to include the cases of unanimous Council voting and special legislative procedures contained in the Protocols in the scope of application of the general bridging clauses of Article 48(7) TEU.

A list of cases in which the Council decides by unanimity or where the Council adopts a legislative act in accordance with a special legislative procedure can be found at the end of Sect. 2.2.

2.2 Exceptions

The wide scope of application of the general bridging clauses of Article 48(7) TEU is subject to a number of exceptions, most of which are explicitly listed in Article 353 TFEU. According to this provision, Article 48(7) TEU shall not apply to four specific cases. In addition, one can identify two cases in which the bridging clause changing the voting requirements in the Council cannot be applied due to opposing constitutional principles. This means that in those situations, without formal Treaty amendment there can be no transition to qualified majority voting in the Council or, as the case may be, to the ordinary legislative procedure (Table 2.1).

2.2.1 Written Exceptions (Article 353 TFEU)

The first exception in Article 353 TFEU applies to paragraphs 3 and 4 of Article 311 TFEU concerning the own resources decision of the Union. According to Article 311(3) TFEU, the Council, acting in accordance with a special legislative procedure, shall unanimously and after consulting the European Parliament adopt a decision laying down the provisions relating to the system of own resources of the Union. As it touches upon a very sensitive matter, that decision shall not enter into force until it is approved by the Member States in accordance with their respective constitutional requirements. It constitutes an atypical decision with primary law

---

[2]See also Hofstötter, in von der Groeben et al. (2015), Artikel 51 EUV, para. 8; Dörr, in Grabitz et al. (2011), Artikel 51 EUV, para. 27.

Table 2.1 Situations where a special legislative procedure and/or unanimity in the Council apply

Legal basis	Legislative procedure	Council	European Parliament	Remarks
TEU				
Article 24(1)(2)/ Article 31(1)(1)	None	Unanimity	–	General framework for Common Foreign and Security Policy
Article 39	None	Unanimity	–	
Article 41(2)(1)	None	Unanimity	–	
Article 41(2)(2)	None	Unanimity	–	
Article 41(3)(1)	None	Unanimity	Consultation	
Article 42(4)	None	Unanimity	–	General framework for Common Security and Defence Policy
Article 44	None	Unanimity (according to Article 42(4) TEU)	–	
Article 46(6)	None	Unanimity	–	General framework for permanent structured cooperation
Article 49(1)	None	Unanimity	Consent (by absolute majority)	Not covered by the bridging clauses
TFEU				
Article 19(1)	Special	Unanimity	Consent	
Article 21(3)	Special	Unanimity	Consultation	
Article 22(1)	Special	Unanimity	Consultation	
Article 22(2)	Special	Unanimity	Consultation	
Article 23(2)	Special	Qualified majority	Consultation	
Article 25(2)	Special	Unanimity	Consent	
Article 64(3)	Special	Unanimity	Consultation	
Article 65(4)	None	Unanimity	–	
Article 77(3)	Special	Unanimity	Consultation	
Article 81(3)(1)	Special	Unanimity	Consultation	
Article 81(3)(2)	Special	Unanimity	Consultation	Special bridging clause
Article 82(2) (d)	None	Unanimity	Consent	
Article 83(1)(3)	None	Unanimity	Consent	
Article 86(1)	Special	Unanimity	Consent	
Article 87(3)	Special	Unanimity	Consultation	
Article 89	Special	Unanimity	Consultation	
Article 92	None	Unanimity	–	
Article 108(2)(3)	None	Unanimity	–	

(continued)

Table 2.1 (continued)

Legal basis	Legislative procedure	Council	European Parliament	Remarks
Article 113	Special	Unanimity	Consultation	
Article 115	Special	Unanimity	Consultation	
Article 118(2)	Special	Unanimity	Consultation	
Article 126(14)(2)	Special	Unanimity	Consultation	
Article 127(6)	Special	Unanimity	Consultation	
Article 140(3)	None	Unanimity	–	Euro area members plus Member State concerned
Article 153(2)(3) in conjunction with Article 153 (1) (c), (d), (f), (g)	Special	Unanimity	Consultation	Subject to special bridging clause of Article 153(2)(4)
Article 153(2)(4)	None	Unanimity	Consultation	Special bridging clause
Article 155(2)(2)	None	Unanimity (if required by Article 153(2))	Information	
Article 182(4)	Special	Qualified majority	Consultation	
Article 192(2)(1)	Special	Unanimity	Consultation	Subject to special bridging clause of Article 192(2)(2)
Article 192(2)(2)	None	Unanimity	Consultation	Special bridging clause
Article 194(3)	Special	Unanimity	Consultation	
Article 203, sentence 1	None	Unanimity	–	
Article 203, sentence 2	Special	Unanimity	Consultation	
Article 207(4)(2)	None	Unanimity (if required for the adoption of internal rules)	Consent or consultation (in accordance with Article 218)	
Article 207(4)(3)	None	Unanimity	Consent or consultation (in accordance with Article 218)	
Article 218(8)(2)	None	Unanimity	Consent or consultation	Approval of the decision on the accession to the ECHR by in accordance with their respective constitutional requirements

(continued)

Table 2.1 (continued)

Legal basis	Legislative procedure	Council	European Parliament	Remarks
Article 219(1)	None	Unanimity	Consultation	
Article 222(3)	None	Unanimity according to Article 31(1) TEU (if defence implications)	Information	
Article 223(1)(2)	Special	Unanimity	Consent (by absolute majority)	Additional approval by Member States in accordance with constitutional requirements
Article 223(2)	Special	Consent (unanimous, if taxation is affected)	Relative majority	As the legislative act is adopted by the European Parliament, not the Council, the general bridging clause that enables a change to the ordinary legislative procedure cannot be applied.
Article 226(3)	Special	Consent (qualified majority)	Relative majority	As the legislative act is adopted by the European Parliament, not the Council, the general bridging clause that enables a change to the ordinary legislative procedure cannot be applied. The other bridging clauses does not apply either, since Council decides by qualified majority anyway.
Article 228(4)	Special	Consent (qualified majority)	Relative majority	As the legislative act is adopted by the European Parliament, not the Council, the general bridging clause that enables a change to the ordinary legislative procedure cannot be applied. The other bridging clause does not apply either, since Council decides by qualified majority anyway.

(continued)

Table 2.1 (continued)

Legal basis	Legislative procedure	Council	European Parliament	Remarks
Article 246(3)	None	Unanimity	–	
Article 252(1)	None	Unanimity	–	
Article 257(4)	None	Unanimity	–	
Article 262	Special	Unanimity	Consultation	
Article 293(1)	None	Unanimity	Consultation	General rule for amending Commission proposals; application of general bridging clause implicitly excluded
Article 294(9)	None	Unanimity	Consultation	General rule for ordinary legislative procedure; application of general bridging clause implicitly excluded
Article 301(2)	None	Unanimity	–	
Article 305(2)	None	Unanimity	–	
Article 308(3) in conjunction with Protocol No. 5	Special	Unanimity	Consultation	
Article 311(3)	Special	Unanimity	Consultation	Application of general bridging clauses excluded by Article 353
Article 311(4)	Special	Qualified majority	Consent	Application of general bridging clauses excluded by Article 353
Article 312(2)(1)	Special	Unanimity	Consent (by absolute majority)	Application of general bridging clauses excluded by Article 353, but special bridging clause in Article 312(2)(2)
Article 314	Special	Qualified majority	Relative or absolute majority	As the legislative act is not adopted by the Council, the general bridging clause that enables a change to the ordinary legislative procedure cannot be applied. The other bridging clause does not apply either, since the Council decides by qualified majority anyway.

(continued)

Table 2.1 (continued)

Legal basis	Legislative procedure	Council	European Parliament	Remarks
Article 329(2)	None	Unanimity	Information	
Article 331(2)	None	Unanimity	–	Only Council representatives of participating Member States
Article 332	None	Unanimity	Consultation	
Article 333(1)	None	Unanimity	–	Special bridging clause for enhanced cooperation
Article 333(2)	None	Unanimity	Consultation	Special bridging clause for enhanced cooperation
Article 342	None	Unanimity	–	
Article 346(2)	None	Unanimity	–	
Article 349	Special	Unanimity	Consultation	
Article 352(1)	Special	Unanimity	Consent	Application of general bridging clause excluded by Article 353
Protocols[a]				
Article 64(1) of Protocol No. 3	None	Unanimity	Consultation	
Article 64(2) of Protocol No. 3	None	Unanimous consent	–	
Article 6 of Protocol No. 13	None	Unanimity	Consultation	
Article 4 of Protocol No. 19	None	Unanimity	–	Only Schengen group plus MS concerned
Article 6(1) of Protocol No. 19	None	Unanimity	–	
Article 6(2) of Protocol No. 19	None	Unanimity	–	Only Schengen group
Article 5 of Protocol No. 21	None	Unanimity	Consultation	
Article 9 of the Annex to Protocol No. 22	None	Unanimity	Consultation	
Article 6(1) of Protocol No. 31	None	Unanimity	Consultation	
Article 2(1) of Protocol No. 37	Special	Qualified majority	Consent	

[a]While not mentioned explicitly, the general bridging clauses are applicable as the Protocols form an integral part of the Treaties.

character.[3] Under paragraph 4 of that Article the Council, acting by means of regulations in accordance with a special legislative procedure, shall, after obtaining the consent of the European Parliament, lay down implementing measures for the Union's own resources system in so far as this is provided for in the decision adopted on the basis of the third paragraph. In the absence of a provision to the contrary, the Council will vote by the default voting rule of Article 16(3) TEU, i.e. by qualified majority. The exclusion of the general bridging clauses underlines the national reservations of sovereignty in budgetary matters;[4] the "power of the purse" of the supranational level is limited to the framework set by the Member States.

The exclusion of the bridging clauses to the implementing measures under paragraph 4 of Article 311 TFEU could be circumvented by having recourse to Article 322(2) TFEU, which is not part of the list of Article 353 TFEU. However, this potential "circumvention" would run dry since under Article 322(2) TFEU, where the Council decides by qualified majority, the legal acts foreseen are not adopted in a (special) legislative procedure and thus no transition (and hence equal parliamentary participation) to the ordinary legislative procedure is possible (see above).

The second exception to Article 48(7) TEU is also located within the financial provisions of the Treaties. Article 353 TFEU excludes the application of the general bridging clauses for the adoption of the multiannual financial framework under the first subparagraph of Article 312(2) TFEU. According to that provision, The Council, acting in accordance with a special legislative procedure, shall adopt the regulation laying down the multiannual financial framework. For that matter, it shall act unanimously after obtaining the consent of the European Parliament, which shall be given by a majority of its component members. However, the second subparagraph of Article 312(2) TFEU contains a special bridging clause for the transition to qualified majority voting in the Council (see Sect. 3.1.4 below).

Furthermore, the application of the general bridging clause shall be excluded for the use of the so called flexibility clause of Article 352 TFEU. According to this "lacuna-filling competence" if action by the Union should prove necessary, within the framework of the policies defined in the Treaties, to attain one of the objectives set out in the Treaties, and the Treaties have not provided the necessary powers, the Council, acting unanimously on a proposal from the Commission and after obtaining the consent of the European Parliament, shall adopt the appropriate measures. Where the measures in question are adopted by the Council in accordance with a special legislative procedure, it shall also act unanimously on a proposal from the Commission and after obtaining the consent of the European Parliament. This provision lies in the outskirts of what is still covered by the

---

[3]Waldhoff, in Calliess and Ruffert (2016), Artikel 311 AEUV, para. 5; see also Bieber, in von der Groeben et al. (2015), Artikel 311 AEUV, para. 14, according to whom the own resources decision, as decision implementing the Treaties, is hierarchically inferior to primary law but due to its binding character on the institutions superior to ordinary secondary law.

[4]Winkler, in Grabitz et al. (2012), Artikel 353 AEUV, para. 11; cf. also Franzius, in Pechstein et al. (2017), Artikel 353 AEUV, para. 5.

principle of conferred competences. While the flexibility clause can be used to fill lacunas in competences already conferred on the Union, it cannot serve as a basis to extend the Union's competences. This is only possible using the ordinary revision procedure of Article 48(1) to (5) TEU.[5] The Member States underlined this fact in Declaration No. 42 to the Treaties, stating that "in accordance with the settled case law of the Court of Justice of the European Union, Article 352 [TFEU], being an integral part of an institutional system based on the principle of conferred powers, cannot serve as a basis for widening the scope of Union powers beyond the general framework created by the provisions of the Treaties as a whole and, in particular, by those that define the tasks and the activities of the Union. In any event, this Article cannot be used as a basis for the adoption of provisions whose effect would, in substance, be to amend the Treaties without following the procedure which they provide for that purpose." However, it can be hard to draw a line. The flexibility clause could easily turn into a Trojan horse and encroach on the Member States' competences. With unanimity required for a decision in the Council, each Member State can veto such legal act, thus giving them a safeguard against a creeping loss in competences and sovereignty.[6] It has to be added that the Lisbon Treaty created special legal bases for many measures that previously had to be adopted on the basis of the flexibility clause (former Article 308 of the EC Treaty). These legal bases (and as a result also subsequent amendments of acts adopted according to former Article 308 TEC) may be subject to application of the bridging clause. In the post-Lisbon practice, the Commission seeks to avoid resorting to Article 352 TFEU as much as possible. As a result, most proposals based on Article 352 TFEU so far have been of technical nature and had only minor political importance.[7]

Finally, as the last provision excluded by Article 353 TFEU, the bridging clauses shall not apply to Article 354 TFEU, which lays down the voting modalities for the sanction procedure of Article 7 TEU. Upon closer look, however, one realises that Article 354 TFEU does not provide for any special legislative procedure or for unanimous decision-making in the Council.[8] In fact, this provision does not contain any decision making whatsoever, but only lays down the voting modalities for decisions taken under Article 7 TEU. The reference in Article 353 TFEU to Article 354 TFEU could thus be understood as referring to decisions taken under Article 7 TEU that shall be excluded from the scope of application of the general bridging clauses, but that article does not contain any legislative procedure or unanimous

[5]Cf. on this European Court of Justice, Opinion 2/94, *Accession to the ECHR*, opinion of 28 March 1996, ECLI:EU:C:1996:140, para. 30; Rossi, in Calliess and Ruffert (2016), Artikel 352 AEUV, para. 74.

[6]Cf. Böttner (2016a), p. 506.

[7]With the exception of the Proposal for a Council Regulation on the exercise of the right to take collective action within the context of the freedom of establishment and the freedom to provide services, COM(2012) 130 of 21 March 2012, that was withdrawn by the Commission when it became clear that it would not find unanimous support of the Member States.

[8]Böttner (2016a), p. 506; Cremer, in Calliess and Ruffert (2016), Artikel 353 AEUV, para. 4; Schorkopf, in Grabitz et al. (2011), Artikel 354 AEUV, para. 6.

decision making by the *Council* either. The inclusion of Article 354 TFEU in the list in Article 353 TFEU can be explained as an editorial error when drafting the provisions on the bridging clauses and their exceptions and transposing them from the failed Constitutional Treaty into the Treaty of Lisbon.[9] Furthermore, it underlines the character of Article 353 as a provision that reflects the fear of the Member States of a creeping and uncontrolled loss on sovereignty and influence and thus is more of a political and symbolic value.[10] For legal purposes, however, the reference to Article 354 TFEU is obsolete.

2.2.2 *Unwritten Exceptions*

One may wonder if the list of exceptions included in Article 353 TFEU is exhaustive or if there are further cases that are not explicitly listed but which, by their very nature, exclude the application of the general bridging clauses. We argue that such cases exist, even though they are admittedly rather limited in number, but nonetheless fundamental in meaning.

An unwritten exception applies to Article 293(1) TFEU. According to that provision and as a general rule, where, pursuant to the Treaties, the Council acts on a proposal from the Commission, it may amend that proposal only by acting unanimously and not by its default voting rule of qualified majority (Article 16(3) TEU). The reason behind this modification is the idea that a proposal originating from the Commission is in accordance with the Union's interest, as the Commission's genuine task is to promote the general interest of the Union and take appropriate initiatives to that end (Article 17(1) sentence 1 TEU).[11] The Commission is to ensure that the general interests of the Union take precedence over individual interest of the Member States in the supranational legislative procedure. This is supported by Article 238(2) TFEU, according to which the qualified majority is subject to a higher threshold in cases where the Council does not act on a proposal from the Commission or from the High Representative of the Union for Foreign Affairs and Security Policy. In those cases, the qualified majority shall be defined as at least 72% of the members of the Council, representing Member States comprising at least 65% of the population of the Union. At the same time, the Commission can use its position under Article 293(1) TFEU in order to protect the interest of individual Member States against an overwhelming majority of other Union members.[12] If the Commission regards certain amendments as running

[9]Meng, in von der Groeben et al. (2015), Artikel 353 AEUV, para. 4.

[10]Franzius, in Pechstein et al. (2017), Artikel 353 AEUV, para. 3.

[11]Cf. Martenczuk, in Grabitz et al. (2015), Artikel 17 EUV, para. 10–14; Adam, in Tizzano (2014), Articolo 293 TFUE, para. II.1.

[12]Cf. Stancanelli, in Curti Gialdino (2012), Articolo 293 TFUE, p. 2104; Adam, in Tizzano (2014), Articolo 293 TFUE, para. II.1; Härtel (2006), § 18 para. 9.

counter to the Union's interests and disagrees with the Council, any Member State is granted a veto position for these amendments even if the legal basis provides for qualified majority voting.[13] On the other hand, Article 293(1) TFEU underlines the Member States' position as the "masters of the Treaties", as Commission proposals can be amended if all Member States agree (unanimity in the Council).[14] However, Article 293(1) TFEU serves an important purpose in the institutional balance of the Union. Changing modalities by means of an act of secondary law would severely disturb the institutional framework and thus can be subject only to the ordinary revision procedure. Furthermore, the rule of Article 293(1) TFEU can hardly be considered an "area" or a "case" in the sense of Article 48(7) TEU, which can be modified by the passerelle clauses. Therefore, although not explicitly mentioned, the bridging clauses do not apply to Article 293(1) TFEU.

A similar situation arises with regard to Article 294(9) TFEU. Article 294 of the TFEU spells out the details of the ordinary legislative procedure and paragraph 9 refers to one aspect of the second reading. If no agreement is reached between the European Parliament and the Council in the first reading (paragraphs 3 through 6), the European Parliament may, within three months, approve the Council's first reading position (by consent or by not acting), reject the Council's position entirely, or propose new amendments (paragraph 7). In the latter case, Parliament's second reading opinion shall be transferred to the Commission for an opinion and to the Council for further action (approval or convening of the Conciliation Committee, paragraph 8). It shall act by qualified majority, but it must act unanimously on the amendments on which the Commission has delivered a negative opinion (paragraph 9). This ties back to the general rule of Article 293(1) TFEU that amendments to Commission proposals are subject to unanimity in the Council. While the Commission can no longer make amendments to its original proposal at that stage of the procedure, the consent (positive opinion) to proposals for amendment in Parliament's second reading opinion has the same effect.[15] The exclusion of paragraph 9 of Article 294 TFEU from the application of the bridging clause is therefore justified by the same reasons of safeguarding the institutional balance that apply to Article 293(1) TFEU.

2.3 "Area" or "Case"

The bridging clause of subparagraph 1 shall apply to given "areas" (DE: *Bereich*; FR: *domaine*) or "cases" (DE: *bestimmter Fall*; FR: *cas déterminé*) in the TFEU or Title V of the TEU, where the Council decides by unanimity. When the bridging clause refers to a given area in which the Council decides by unanimity, it refers to

[13] Böttner (2016b), p. 107.
[14] Cf. Hetmeier, in Lenz and Borchardt (2012), Artikel 293 AEUV, para. 4.
[15] Böttner (2016b), p. 114 f.

situations in which an entire policy area is subject to unanimous Council voting. This is the case for the Common Foreign and Security Policy covered by Title V of the TEU.

Where the bridging clause refers to certain "cases" of unanimous decision making in the Council, it refers to individual Treaty provisions that provide for unanimity in the Council, i.e. to specific legal bases. Logically, subparagraph 2 concerning the applicable legislative procedure does not contain any such distinction between "area" and "case", as any legislative procedure provided for in the Treaties only covers a certain case of decision-making. Activating the bridging clause for a certain legal basis would mean that all future legal acts shall be adopted by qualified majority in the Council or the ordinary legislative procedure.

In this regard, the bridging clause does not necessarily change the entire legal basis. Instead, the decision activating a bridging clause can specify a very narrow area of competence. For example, a bridging clause could be activated for spatial planning, but limited to areas near state borders—Article 192(2)(b), first bullet point, TFEU (but limited to border areas), while not covering spatial planning in general, or all cases under Article 192(2)(b), or 192(2) TFEU as a whole. Admittedly, this may lead to difficulties determining the applicable procedure for a given legal act based on the modified legal basis.

While the *ratio* of the bridging clauses is to shift intergovernmental to supranational voting rules, one may wonder if the bridging clauses could also be used for *individual* cases of decision making, i.e. for a single legal or legislative project. In accordance with the wording of Article 48(7) TEU, especially with regard to other language versions, this situation could be understood as an individual "case". Frankly, at a first glance this may seem illogical. Why would the European Council unanimously authorise the Council to adopt a single legal act by qualified majority if obviously the Council could have adopted it also by unanimity, as apparently consensus was reached between the Member States. However, granting the Council the right to proceed with qualified majority can make sense for future amendments of the legal act. Moreover, there can be an interest to give co-decision rights to the European Parliament for a single legislative project without having a general shift to the ordinary legislative procedure under a certain legal basis. Therefore, the *passerelle* clauses can also be used for an individual case in the sense of a single legal project. For that matter, the European Council decision activating the bridging clause must contain a description of the legal project for which the *passerelle* will apply. This could be done with reference to a Commission proposal. Again, a problem with the applicability of the bridging clause decision to an individual case may arise if the scope of the Commission proposal, for which the bridging clause was activated, is changed (especially broadened) in the course of the legislative procedure. The same applies to future amendments that would extend the scope of the original act by adding further related issues to its ambit. Therefore it is advisable that the European Council decision be as precise as possible, should the bridging clause be activated regarding individual cases or regarding parts of legal bases below the resolution provided by the wording of the Treaty (e.g. the aforementioned example on spatial planning in borderlands only). The European Council decision should also expressly state that the bridging clause is being activated both for the envisaged proposal as well as for its future amendments.

2.4 Relationship Between the Two General Bridging Clauses

The wording of Article 48(7) TEU does not readily reveal the relationship between the two individual bridging clauses contained therein. The second subparagraph applies to situations where to Treaties contain a "special legislative procedure". A special legislative procedure is the adoption of a regulation, directive or decision by the European Parliament with the participation of the Council, or by the latter with the participation of the European Parliament (Article 289(2) TFEU). The voting modalities for both the European Parliament and the Council are laid down in the individual cases. As mentioned, the *passerelle* of Article 48(7)(2) TEU only applies to the second case ("acts to be adopted by the Council"). The wording suggests that, *whenever* the TFEU provides for a legislative act to be adopted by the Council by a special legislative procedure, *only* the bridging clause of subparagraph 2 can be activated. This would mean that in case of a special legislative procedure, flexibility in the form of a bridging clause could only be used to pass to the ordinary legislative procedure.

In the majority of the cases, a special legislative procedure entails that the Council, according to the explicit wording of the respective provision, shall decide by a unanimous vote.[16] Hence, those voting procedures are not only a special legislative procedure, but also contain a unanimous Council decision, which is covered by the first subparagraph of Article 48(7) TEU, i.e. the other general bridging clause ("where the Treaty [...] provides for the Council to act by unanimity"). As a consequence, where the Treaty provides for a special legislative procedure with unanimous Council voting, either of the *passerelles* can be used. The two bridging clauses are not mutually exclusive.[17]

---

[16]Exceptions are Article 23(2) and Article 182(4) TFEU, which provide for the adoption of a legislative act by the Council according to a special legislative procedure, without, however, requiring unanimity in the Council. As a result, the Council in these cases will act by the default voting rule of qualified majority according to Article 16(3) TEU. The same is true for Article 311 (4) TFEU, but the application of the general bridging clauses of Article 48(7) TEU shall be excluded. Likewise, Article 312(2)(1) TFEU provides for the adoption of a legislative act by the Council, acting unanimously in accordance with a special legislative procedure, but the application of Article 48(7) TEU shall be excluded. However, a special bridging clause applies that allows at least a transition to qualified majority voting in the Council. For the adoption of the act provided for in Article 314 TFEU, a special legislative procedure with qualified majority voting in the Council shall apply, but the act is not adopted by the Council, but in cooperation with the European Parliament.

[17]Böttner (2016a), p. 509; Peers (2012), p. 46; with a different view Öhlinger and Potacs (2014), p. 26.

This means that in those cases, the European Council can authorise the Council to act by qualified majority without granting the European Parliament the right to legislate on equal footing as co-legislator. Despite the transition from unanimity to qualified majority in the Council, the European Parliament would continue to participate by consultation or consent. The legislative procedure would thus remain a "special" legislative procedure in the sense of Article 289(2) TFEU. While this holds true from a legal point of view, the European Parliament could use its power in the procedure for the activation of the bridging clause and refuse to give its consent if it is put in a disadvantage. Also, the national Parliaments could use their veto power to prevent such parliamentary discrimination.

2.5 Legal Effects, Revocability and Judicial Review

2.5.1 Legal Effects

Once a bridging clause has been activated by decision of the European Council, a certain area or case will from then on be subject to qualified majority voting in the Council and/or the ordinary legislative procedure. This is irrespective of the fact to what degree the European Parliament was included under the special legislative procedure (information, consultation, consent). Also, one must keep in mind that the bridging clause does not necessarily change the legal basis as a whole, but the European Council can specify to which aspects of the legal basis they shall apply (see Sect. 2.3).

Qualified majority voting in the Council (Article 16(3) TEU)[18] and the co-decision procedure between the Council and the European Parliament (Article 289(1), Article 294 TFEU) have become the default procedures under the Treaty of Lisbon. Thus, by using the bridging clauses the remaining special modalities can be transferred to the default procedures without having to resort to the ordinary Treaty revision procedure. What is common to both alternatives is the departure from the requirement of voting by unanimity in the Council.[19] This entails for the individual Member State (via their Council representative) the loss of the unconditional veto position or, in other words, the introduction of the possibility for the individual Member State to be outvoted. Vetoes are henceforth only possible if at least four members oppose a decision (blocking minority, if a qualified majority is assumed, Article 16(4)(2) of the TEU) or, if a formal vote is taken, the number of opposing states prevents either or both of the 65% and 55% requirement. In the words of the

[18]While the Council may adopt decisions by qualified majority vote once a bridging clause is activated, one should note, however, that according to Article 293(1) TFEU the Council will still need unanimity to amend a Commission proposal. See on this Böttner (2016b), p. 113.

[19]German Federal Constitutional Court, 2 BvR 2728/13 et al., *Treaty of Lisbon*, judgment of 30 June 2009, ECLI:DE:BVerfG:2009:es20090630.2bve000208, para. 316; Streinz et al. (2010), p. 53 f.; Cremer, in Calliess and Ruffert (2016), Artikel 48 EUV, para. 12.

German Federal Constitutional Court, majority decisions in the Council that are not agreed upon by a formal revision of the Treaties constitute "drops in influence" (*Einflussknicke*) that may lower the level of the democratic legitimation of acts of the European public authority.[20] The enhanced role of the European Parliament (if this passerelle is used) may provide compensation with regard to democratic legitimation. However, from the perspective of national law, this may result in the requirement for enhanced safeguards to ensure democratic legitimation (see Sect. 4.5).[21]

Furthermore, the activation of the bridging clause does not only change the voting modalities, but more comprehensively all details that are related to this shift. For example, Article 46(6) TEU provides that certain decisions and recommendations of the Council within the framework of permanent structured cooperation shall be adopted by unanimity and that unanimity shall be constituted by the votes of the representatives of the participating Member States only. If the bridging clause were to be activated for this provision, shifting from unanimity to qualified majority, the reference in sentence 2 of Article 46(6) TEU should read that the qualified majority applies to the participating Member States. A similar situation is found in Article 140(3) TFEU on the abrogation of the derogation from the provisions of the Economic and Monetary Union. For reason of clarity, the European Council decision should contain this reference.

On the other hand, the general bridging clauses of Article 48(7) TEU can be used only to change the voting modalities in the Council or the applicable legislative procedure. Further amendments to the Treaties, especially on the distribution of competences as well as the scope of and arrangements for exercising the Union's competences (cf. Article 2(6) TFEU) are not possible.[22] Only to that extent the bridging clauses may be used to bypass national procedures of consent or ratification of Treaty amendments.[23] The limited scope of application justifies substituting the ratification requirement by the possibility for national Parliaments to veto an initiative. Fundamental changes to the Treaties are reserved to the Convention method and the ordinary revision procedure or, as the case may be, to the simplified procedure of Article 48(6) TEU. Only these procedures can confer the necessary level of democratic legitimation.[24]

What they cannot change either is the participation in the decision-making procedure of any other bodies or committees foreseen by the Treaties. The *ratio legis* of the bridging clauses is to facilitate decision making, hence it only applies to

[20]German Federal Constitutional Court, 2 BvR 2728/13 et al., *OMT*, judgment of 21 June 2016, ECLI:DE:BVerfG:2016:rs20160621.2bvr272813, para. 131.

[21]Wendel (2011), p. 225.

[22]Peers (2012), p. 41 f.; Böttner (2016a), p. 503.

[23]Grard, in Burgorgue-Larsen et al. (2007), Article IV-444, para. 2.

[24]German Federal Constitutional Court, 2 BvR 2728/13 et al., *Treaty of Lisbon*, judgment of 30 June 2009, ECLI:DE:BVerfG:2009:es20090630.2bve000208, para. 309; Terhechte (2008), p. 169; Granat (2016), p. 73; Böttner (2016a), p. 501.

the institutions actually taking the decisions (Council, European Parliament). It leaves unaffected the consultative role of, for example, the Committee of Regions or the Economic and Social Committee.

Moreover, the decision to activate a bridging clause changes primary law (hence a "simplified *revision* procedure") by modifying the legal basis for the adoption of a legal or legislative act. For the sake of clarity and transparency, any legal act adopted on the basis of a Treaty provision that has been modified by a passerelle clause should contain a short reference to this fact in the recitals, indicating also the (European) Council decision activating the passerelle.[25]

Furthermore, the use of the passerelle clauses is monodirectional. They can only be used to shift to qualified majority voting in the Council or the ordinary legislative procedure in the cases in which the text of the Treaties (as amended by the Treaty of Lisbon) provide for unanimous Council voting or a special legislative procedure. They cannot be used in the other direction, i.e. from qualified majority to unanimity or for installing a special legislative procedure where the Treaties establish the ordinary legislative procedure. The only exception is the case that a decision to activate a bridging clause is revoked (see Sect. 2.5.2).

In addition, the legal effect of the second passerelle regarding the legislative procedure is limited to *changing* a special into the ordinary legislative procedure. It will not be possible to use this passerelle in order to *introduce* a (the ordinary) legislative procedure if the text of the Treaties does not already provide for one. This means that it is not possible to turn a procedure for the adoption of only a *legal* act into a procedure for the adoption of a *legislative* act. This distinction is relevant in the light of Article 289(3) TFEU which provides that legal acts adopted by legislative procedure shall constitute legislative acts: According to Article 17(2) TEU, as a general rule, legislative acts may only be adopted on the basis of a Commission proposal, other legal acts only if the Treaties so provide. In addition, in contrast to procedures leading to the adoption of mere legal act, legislative procedures always (in one form or the other) involve the European Parliament (see Article 289(1) and (2) TFEU). Furthermore, from a strictly legal point of view, the scrutiny of national Parliaments under Protocols No. 1 and 2 applies only to draft *legislative* acts.[26]

---

[25]The recital of the legal act should read, for example:

> Having regard to Treaty on the Functioning of the European Union, and in particular Article 194(3) thereof, as modified by Decision No. xxx/2017 of the European Council
>
> (…) On 3 October 2017 the European Council adopted the Decision No. xxx/2017 on the basis of Article 48(7) of the Treaty on European Union, providing that decisions under Article 194(3) of the Treaty on the Functioning of the European Union shall henceforth be subject to the ordinary legislative procedure.

[26]See Article 2 of Protocol No. 1 on the role of national Parliaments in the European Union and Article 3 of Protocol No. 2 on the application of the principles of subsidiarity and proportionality.

As a general rule, once a bridging clause is activated it applies to all areas or cases as specified in the European Council decision. This means that legal or legislative acts adopted on the basis of a Treaty provision that has been subject to a passerelle may be amended, repealed or replaced only by the same procedure, i.e. the Treaty provision (legal basis) as modified by the bridging clause.

2.5.2 Revocability

The question further arises if and under which conditions the decision to activate a bridging clause can be revoked. According to the theory of *actus contrarius*, the competence to adopt a legal act entails also the competence to repeal that act by the same authority under the same procedure. For the bridging clauses this means that an activated bridging clause can be deactivated by a European Council decision. This, however, leads to two questions:

First, one may wonder if the decision to deactivate a bridging clause really has to follow all procedural steps as the decision to activate the passerelle. If that was the case, all national Parliaments could veto the repeal of a bridging clause and thus in essence could veto the gaining back of a veto position of the national Council representative, since unanimity in the Council would be restored. This seems paradoxical. On the other hand, the procedure under Article 48(7) TEU also requires the consent of the European Parliament. At least for the passerelle that changes the special into the ordinary legislative procedure, the position of the European Parliament improves with the activation of the clause or, vice versa, worsens if the passerelle is revoked.

This is connected with the second questions: Is there a sort of "grandfathering" for legal acts adopted under a passerelle? The question arises when legal acts are adopted under an activated passerelle which later is revoked. The first possibility is that any amendment to or the repeal of hat legal act would now be subject to the special legislative procedure or unanimity in the Council as originally foreseen by the Treaties. The repeal of the decision activating the bridging clause would have the effect as though it had never been activated in the first place. *Any* legal act adopted on the legal basis in question would thus be subject to unanimity in the Council and/or to the special legislative procedure. The second option is that those legal acts that have been adopted under a bridging clause will continue to be subject to this clause for any future amendment or repeal, while new legal acts would fall under the original procedure. The repeal of the decision activating the bridging clause would have an effect for *future* legal acts only.

As a general rule, the adoption, repeal or amendment of a legal act is subject to the procedure foreseen in the Treaties at the time the legislative institutions act. This

---

See also Böttner (2016c), p. 510 f. The parliamentary scrutiny of drafts of other legal (i.e. non-legislative) acts has its basis in national law.

holds true even if the legal basis changes over time as the result of a Treaty revision. Provided that the procedure for the repeal of a decision activating a bridging clause is the same as for the original adoption (*actus contrarius*), there is no reason why it should be any different in this case. The European Parliament can safeguard its acquired rights from the shift to the ordinary legislative procedure by not giving its consent to the repeal of the passerelle.

2.5.3 Judicial Review

Lastly, we will take a look on the issue of judicial review. Generally speaking, the European Court of Justice is competent to interpret the Treaties, i.e. primary law, but cannot decide on the validity of primary law provisions (cf. Article 267 TFEU). However, while the legal effect is to change primary law, the activation of a bridging clause is based on a decision of the European Council, hence an act of secondary law. The European Court of Justice is competent to rule on the validity and interpretation of acts of the institutions, bodies, offices or agencies of the Union (Article 267(1)(b) TFEU). This includes the review whether all requirements and procedural elements for the adoption of an act have been complied with, since the Court shall ensure that in the interpretation and application of the Treaties the law is observed (Article 19(1)(1), sentence 1, of the TEU). Thus, European Council decisions under Article 48(7) TEU are subject to judicial review.[27]

References

Böttner R (2016a) The treaty amendment procedures and the relationship between Article 31(3) TEU and the general bridging clause of Article 48(7) TEU. Eur Const Law Rev 499–521

Böttner R (2016b) Ein scharfes Schwert der Kommission? Überlegungen zu Artikel 293 AEUV. Europarecht 105–122

Böttner R (2016c) Eine Idee lernt laufen—zur Praxis der Verstärkten Zusammenarbeit nach Lissabon. Zeitschrift für europarechtliche Studien 501–549

Burgorgue-Larsen L, Levade A, Picod F (eds) (2007) Traité établissant une Constitution pour l'Europe, Partie I et IV. Bruylant, Brussels

Calliess C, Ruffert M (eds) (2016) EUV/AEUV, 5th edn. C.H.Beck, Munich

Curti Gialdino C (ed) (2012) Codice dell'Unione europea operativo. TUE e TFUE commentati articolo per articolo. Simone, Naples

Grabitz E, Hilf M, Nettesheim M (eds) (2009 ff.) Das Recht der Europäischen Union: EUV/ AEUV. loose leaf. C.H.Beck, Munich

[27]See, with regard to the European Council decision amending Article 136 TFEU, European Court of Justice, Case C-370/12, *Pringle*, ECLI:EU:C:2012:756, para. 33 ff.; see also Nettesheim (2006), p. 742; Böttner (2016a), p. 509. Cf. also Czech Constitutional Court, Pl. US 19/08, *Treaty of Lisbon I*, decision of 26 November 2008, ECLI:CZ:US:2008:Pl.US.19.08.1, para. 162 ff.

Granat K (2016) Interparliamentary cooperation and the simplified revision procedures. In: Lupo N, Fasone C (eds) Interparliamentary cooperation in the composite European constitution. Hart, Oxord, pp 73–90

Härtel I (2006) Handbuch Europäische Rechtsetzung. Springer, Heidelberg

Lenz C-O, Borchardt KD (eds) (2012) EU-Verträge, Kommentar. Bundesanzeiger Verlag, Bonn

Nettesheim M (2006) Normenhierarchien im EU-Recht. Europarecht 737–772

Öhlinger T, Potacs M (2014) EU-Recht und staatliches Recht, 5th edn. LexisNexis, Vienna

Pechstein M, Nowak C, Häde U (eds) (2017) Frankfurter Kommentar zu EUV, GRC und AEUV. Mohr Siebeck, Tübingen

Peers S (2012) The future of EU Treaty amendments. Yearb Eur Law 17–111

Streinz R, Ohler C, Herrmann C (2010) Der Vertrag von Lissabon zur Reform der EU, 2nd edn. C.H.Beck, Munich

Terhechte JP (2008) Der Vertrag von Lissabon: Grundlegende Verfassungsurkunde der europäischen Rechtsgemeinschaft oder technischer Änderungsvertrag? Europarecht 143–189

Tizzano A (ed) (2014) Trattati dell'Unione europea. Guiffrè, Milan

von der Groeben H, Schwarze J, Hatje A (eds) (2015) Europäisches Unionsrecht, 7th edn. Nomos, Baden-Baden

Wendel M (2011) Permeabilität im europäischen Verfassungsrecht. Mohr Siebeck, Tübingen

Chapter 3
Special Bridging Clauses

Apart from the general bridging clauses of Article 48(7) TEU, the Treaties contain a number of provisions by virtue of which the legislative procedure or the voting modalities for a specific area can be modified without the need to have recourse to the ordinary Treaty revision procedure. As mentioned above (Sect. 1.3), even before the entry into force of the Treaty of Lisbon, the instrument of bridging clauses, i.e. of amending voting procedures by means of an act of secondary law, was not unknown to European constitutional law. However, the Treaty of Lisbon significantly added to the existing rules by introducing the general bridging clauses of Article 48(7) TEU as well as a number of specific passerelles. These latter clauses shall be covered in the following sections.

3.1 Sector-Specific Bridging Clauses

3.1.1 Social Policy

A passerelle was included already in ex-Article 137(2)(2) of the EC Treaty and is now found in Article 153(2)(4) of the TFEU in the Title on social policy. According to this provision, the European Parliament and the Council, acting in accordance with the ordinary legislative procedure after consulting the Economic and Social Committee and the Committee of the Regions shall encourage cooperation between the Member States and may adopt directives containing minimum requirements for gradual implementation in a number of fields listed in paragraph 1 of Article 153 TFEU [lit. (a) through lit. (k)] in order to achieve the objectives of the Union's social policy as spelled out in Article 151 TFEU. Certain fields, however, shall be subject to a special legislative procedure with unanimity in the Council and consultation of the European Parliament and the Committees. This applies to social security and social protection of workers [lit. (c)], protection of workers where their

R. Böttner and J. Grinc, *Bridging Clauses in European Constitutional Law*,
SpringerBriefs in Law, https://doi.org/10.1007/978-3-319-73341-8_3

employment contract is terminated [lit. (d)], representation and collective defence of the interests of workers and employers, including co-determination, but excluding pay, the right of association, the right to strike or the right to impose lock-outs [lit. (f)] and conditions of employment for third-country nationals legally residing in Union territory [lit. (g)]. By using a passerelle contained in that Article, the ordinary legislative procedure can be rendered applicable for the areas listed in lit. (d), (f) and (g).

Social security and social protection of workers [lit. (c)] is not included in the enumeration. Thus, the passerelle of Article 153 TFEU does not apply to this element of law-making in social policy. This shows that social security is still a sensitive area for the Member States for which they are reluctant to transfer sovereign rights to the European Union.[1] Changing to qualified majority in the Council or to the ordinary legislative procedure requires activating the general bridging clauses of Article 48(7) TEU.

The decision to activate the bridging clause under Article 153(2) TFEU is taken by the Council, acting unanimously on a proposal from the Commission, after consulting the European Parliament.

3.1.2 Environmental Policy

A second passerelle clause that existed pre-Lisbon was the one in Article 175(2)(2) of the EC Treaty on environmental policy. With the Treaty of Lisbon, the provision was transferred and the bridging clause is now found in Article 192(2)(2) TFEU. On the basis of Article 192(1) TFEU, the European Parliament and the Council, acting in accordance with the ordinary legislative procedure and after consulting the Economic and Social Committee and the Committee of the Regions, shall decide what action is to be taken by the Union in order to achieve the objectives of the Union's environmental policy laid down in Article 191 TFEU. By way of derogation from this general rule, the Council acting unanimously and after consulting the European Parliament, the Economic and Social Committee and the Committee of the Regions, shall adopt certain measures in accordance with a special legislative procedure (Article 192(2)(1) TFEU). These include provisions primarily of a fiscal nature [lit. (a)], measures affecting town and country planning, quantitative management of water resources or affecting, directly or indirectly, the availability of those resources, and land use, with the exception of waste management [lit. (b)], as well as measures significantly affecting a Member State's choice between different energy sources and the general structure of its energy supply [lit. (c)]. All of these matters concern areas which are sensitive to the Member States' autonomy and therefore, apart from the Union's competence in environmental policy, either the

[1]Langer, in von der Groeben et al. (2015), Artikel 153 AEUV, para. 23.

Union has no legislative powers or unanimity within the Council is required.[2] As is often the case, the required unanimity is the result of a political compromise and a concession to Member States that do not (yet) want to proceed by qualified majority.[3] On the other hand, the passerelle is also a compromise to shift to the ordinary legislative procedure/qualified majority in the Council once all Member States are ready and willing.

As laid down in subparagraph 2, the Council, acting unanimously on a proposal from the Commission and after consulting the European Parliament, the Economic and Social Committee and the Committee of the Regions, may make the ordinary legislative procedure applicable to the matters referred to in the first subparagraph.

3.1.3 Family Law with Cross-Border Implications

A new[4] bridging clause was introduced in the Chapter on judicial cooperation in civil matters. Judicial cooperation in civil matters having cross-border implications shall be based on the principle of mutual recognition of judgments and of decisions in extrajudicial cases. On the basis of Article 81(2) TFEU, the European Parliament and the Council, acting in accordance with the ordinary legislative procedure, shall adopt measures aimed at ensuring, for example, mutual recognition and enforcement between Member States of judgments and of decisions in extrajudicial cases, the cross-border service of judicial and extrajudicial documents or the compatibility of the rules applicable in the Member States concerning conflict of laws and of jurisdiction. However, as paragraph 3(1) of this Article provides, measures concerning family law with cross-border implications shall be established by the Council, acting in accordance with a special legislative procedure. For this purpose, the Council shall act unanimously after consulting the European Parliament. Again, national sovereignty concerns have been the reason for excluding these matters from the default voting procedures,[5] as the legal and cultural traditions in the

[2]European Court of Justice, Case C-36/98, *Spain v. Council*, decision of 30 January 2001, ECLI: EU:C:2001:64, para 54.

[3]Cf. Kahl, in Streinz (2012), Artikel 192 AEUV, para. 17; Krämer, in von der Groeben et al. (2015), Vorbemerkung zu den Artikeln 191 bis 193 AEUV, para. 8 f.

[4]Not exactly a predecessor, Article 67(2) of the EC Treaty contained a provision according to which, after a transitional period of five years following the entry into force of the Treaty of Amsterdam, in which the Council shall act unanimously on a proposal from the Commission or on the initiative of a Member State and after consulting the European Parliament, "the Council, acting unanimously after consulting the European Parliament, shall take a decision with a view to providing for all or parts of the areas covered by this title to be governed by the [co-decision] procedure referred to in Article 251 and adapting the provisions relating to the powers of the Court of Justice".

[5]Kotzur, in Geiger et al. (2017), Artikel 81 AEUV, para. 15.

Member States in the area of family law still differ significantly, e.g. with regard to divorce or same-sex marriage.[6]

Subparagraphs 2 and 3 establish the possibility to determine certain aspects of family law with cross-border implications which may be the subject of acts adopted by the ordinary legislative procedure. The Council, on a proposal from the Commission and acting unanimously after consulting the European Parliament, may adopt a decision determining those aspects. The Commission's proposal shall be notified to the national Parliaments. Each national Parliament has the possibility within six months of the date of notification to oppose and veto the proposal. In that case, the Council shall not adopt the decision.

3.1.4 Multiannual Financial Framework

An additional bridging clause introduced by the Lisbon Treaty reform is found in Article 312 TFEU concerning the multiannual financial framework of the Union, which shall be established for a period of at least five years and which shall be the basis for the Union's annual budget. The regulation laying down the multiannual financial framework shall be adopted by the Council in accordance with a special legislative procedure. The Council shall act unanimously after obtaining the consent of the European Parliament, which shall be given by absolute majority (majority of its component members).

This provision is a peculiar case. As mentioned above, according to Article 353, second indent, of the TFEU, the general bridging clauses shall not apply to this provision. However, the second subparagraph of Article 312(2) TFEU contains a separate bridging clause, according to which the European Council may, unanimously, adopt a decision authorising the Council to act by a qualified majority when adopting the regulation referred to in the first subparagraph. This means that a switch from unanimity to qualified majority in the Council is possible, while the transition to the ordinary legislative procedure is excluded. Hence, it is not possible for the European Parliament to proceed on equal footing with the Council in a co-decision procedure and by its default voting rule (Article 231 TFEU: majority of votes cast).

The possibility for the Council to proceed with qualified majority means that when adopting the decision on the Union's expenditure, Member States can be outvoted. At first glance, it may seem problematic that the national Parliaments have no say in a decision concerning the use of financial means of a supranational organisation that is funded by national resources, as the budgetary right is a core right of parliaments. This could not be prevented by national procedures that make the vote of the national Council representative dependent on a decision of the

[6]Cf. Leible, in Streinz (2012), Artikel 81 AEUV, para. 46; Hoppe, in Lenz and Borchardt (2012), Article 81 AEUV, para. 12; Rossi, in Calliess and Ruffert (2016), Artikel 81 AEUV, para. 35.

national Parliament either. However, this passerelle deals with the decision on the expenditure of resources that have already been granted to the Union by a procedure that provides for parliamentary involvement. According to Article 311(4) TFEU, The Council, acting in accordance with a special legislative procedure, shall unanimously and after consulting the European Parliament adopt a decision laying down the provisions relating to the system of own resources of the Union. In this context it may establish new categories of own resources or abolish an existing category. As mentioned above, the application of the bridging clauses is excluded for the provision, hence the Council will always decide by unanimity, which would leave room for a national mandating system (cf. Sect. 4.5 below). Furthermore, that decision shall not enter into force until it is approved by the Member States in accordance with their respective constitutional requirements, which usually requires national parliamentary consent.

One may wonder why the Treaty makers would include this kind of "double exemption". The original version of Article 54(4) of the draft Treaty establishing a Constitution for Europe provided that only the first multiannual financial framework after the entry into force of the Constitutional Treaty should be adopted by unanimous Council vote. Following that the Council would have acted by qualified majority. However, due to political controversies and opposition by the net contributors for fear of losing influence in the budgetary procedure,[7] the compromise was to include a bridging clause enabling the European Council to shift to qualified majority voting in the Council once political agreement was reached (Article I-55 (4) of the Constitutional Treaty). Under this construction, there would have been a true *lex specialis* for the multiannual financial framework; there was no equivalent to what is now Article 353 TFEU. Under the Treaty of Lisbon, a general exception was included, ruling out any possibility to include the European Parliament via the ordinary legislative procedure. However, while the European Parliament is not involved as co-decider, it can still use the requirement to give its consent to exert political pressure in order to have its position taken into account. There is, therefore, no reason (in a future Treaty revision) to exclude the bridging clause for transition to the ordinary legislative procedure.

3.1.5 Relationship to the General Bridging Clauses

In contrast to the general bridging clauses, which have a universal scope of application (see Sect. 2.1 above), these special clauses can be applied only to individual policy areas and narrow subject matters. In addition, theses clauses provide for a procedure to activate the passerelle that differs from the procedure under Article 48(7) TEU. As a rule of thumb, the decision to make use of these

[7] Waldhoff, in Calliess and Ruffert (2016), Artikel 312 AEUV, para. 8.

passerelles is taken by the Council,[8] in some cases on the basis of a proposal by the Commission,[9] while there is no requirement to obtain the consent of the European Parliament[10] and no veto right for national Parliaments.[11]

These differences raise the question on the relationship of the special bridging clauses to the general bridging clauses of Article 48(7) TEU. In essence, it breaks down to the question of whether the existence of these specific clauses excludes the application of the general clauses or whether they can be used alternatively.

They could constitute *leges speciales* to the general bridging clauses. According to the principle of "lex specialis derogat legi generali", the application of a general provision, i.e. a provision with a general scope, is excluded by a provision with a specific scope. A *lex specialis* exists if a provision covers a certain area that falls within the scope of the general provision, but has a different legal effect.[12] As a consequence, this would mean that, for the policy areas for which a special bridging clause exists, the procedure laid down in these provisions must be followed.

However, in determining whether a provision is an actual *lex specialis* or merely an alternative to the general provision, one must also take into account the intention of the legislator and the *ratio legis* of the special provision. The intention of the sector-specific bridging clauses is to provide for a simplified procedure for a narrow area that may require a more flexible response than the general bridging clause or even the ordinary revision procedure. The intention is not, however, to generally exclude parliamentary participation. Therefore, they do not bar the institutions from using the general passerelles if they feel the need for enhanced legitimation (through parliamentary participation) for such a decision. As a result, the passerelles covered in this section are not *leges speciales* in the strict sense, but rather sector-specific alternatives for the European institutions, namely the Council.[13] The only exception, of course, is Article 312 TFEU, for which the application of the general bridging clauses is explicitly excluded by Article 353 TFEU (see Sect. 2.2.1 above).

3.2 Enhanced Cooperation

The reform of the framework for enhanced cooperation brought about by the Treaty of Lisbon also led to the introduction of special bridging clauses in this area, contained in Article 333 TFEU. The provision states that, with the exception of

---

[8]With the exception of Article 312(2) TFEU, according to which the European Council adopts the decision.

[9]Not under Article 312(2) and Article 333 TFEU.

[10]If anything, the European Parliament is only consulted.

[11]A veto right exists only under Article 81(3)(2) TFEU.

[12]Reimer (2016), para. 204 f.

[13]In an earlier publication, one of the authors prematurely stated that the sector-specific bridging clauses are *leges specialis* to Article 48(7) TEU and thus suggested that they exclude the application of the general procedure. See Böttner (2017), p. 385.

provisions having military or defence implications, the Council, acting by unanimity of the participating Member States, may adopt a decision stipulating that it will act by a qualified majority in cases where a provision of the Treaties which may be applied in the context of enhanced cooperation stipulates that the Council shall act unanimously. Likewise, the Council, acting by unanimity of the participating Member States and after consulting the European Parliament, may adopt a decision stipulating that it will act under the ordinary legislative procedure in cases where a provision of the Treaties which may be applied in the context of enhanced cooperation stipulates that the Council shall adopt acts under a special legislative procedure.

While this provision seems to simply mirror the passerelles of Article 48(7) TEU, a number of questions arises with regard to the relationship to the general bridging clauses. It is obvious that the general bridging clauses can be used to shift to the ordinary legislative procedure or to qualified majority voting in the Council for the use of a provision *in general*, including any existing enhanced cooperation in that area, while the passerelle of Article 333 TFEU can be used only within an enhanced cooperation and only for that particular cooperation, i.e. for the scope and objectives approved by the authorising decision under Article 329 TFEU. It serves as procedural simplification for the members of an individual cooperation. As improbable as it may be, in the case of parallel cooperation on the same subject matter,[14] the activation of the special bridging clauses of Article 333 TFEU would apply only to that group of Member States that has agreed on it. This also means that, in case of adoption of a legislative act by the Union as a whole (precedence of uniform integration[15]), this is subject to the special legislative procedure or unanimity in the Council as stipulated in the Treaties. The activated passerelle in enhanced cooperation would not apply.

At first glance, it may seem unlikely that these passerelle clauses would ever be activated. In practice, enhanced cooperation is used for a narrow scope of action, usually the pursuit of a single legislative project or legislative initiative by a group of willing Member States, because the legal act could not be adopted by the Union as a whole. It would be illogical for the Member States participating in the enhanced cooperation to decide by unanimous vote to not have to decide by unanimity on a specific legal act, but instead by qualified majority. If agreement exists between the participating Member States, they can vote on and adopt the legal act right away.[16]

However, the specific passerelles of Article 333 TFEU can gain relevance in two regards. First, as mentioned above, the use of a bridging clause has an effect on the entire life cycle of legal acts adopted on the respective legal basis, i.e. the adoption and any future amendment or revocation. Member States (or, to be more precise, the

[14]On this, see Böttner (2016b), p. 539.

[15]Böttner (2016b), p. 529 f.; Blanke, in Grabitz et al. (2016), Artikel 20 EUV, para. 57, Becker (1998), p. 53.

[16]Cf. Böttner (2016b), p. 528.

Council) could therefore decide to use a qualified majority for the amendment of legal acts adopted within a given cooperation in order to allow for its dynamic evolution and to prevent a new blocking position of individual Member States that led to the resort to enhanced cooperation in the first place. Second, the establishment of an enhanced cooperation (with the exception within the framework of the Common Foreign and Security Policy) requires the consent of the European Parliament (Article 329(1) TFEU). Parliament could use its veto power to force the Council to make use of the passerelles of Article 333 TFEU so that the European Parliament would be involved in the adoption of a legal act within the cooperation.[17] So far, the European Parliament has not made use of this option, but is well aware of it.[18]

In addition, there is another, even more important uncertainty regarding the relationship between the general and the special bridging clauses for enhanced cooperation. The existence of a special passerelle for enhanced cooperation raises the question of what would happen once all Union Member States accede to an existing cooperation. An established cooperation is open for all Member States to join. In general, the cooperation ends once all Member States have acceded to that cooperation and the legal acts adopted within that cooperation become part of the *acquis communautaire*.[19]

As bridging clauses activated within enhanced cooperation are not merely acts implementing that cooperation, but instead have effects on the primary law, one can distinguish four different scenarios for the fate of these decisions activating a bridging clause once all Union Member States have acceded to an established cooperation:

(1) Due to its peculiar constitutional nature, the decision activating a bridging clause will cease to be in force. This means that any amendment, including the annulment, of legal acts adopted within enhanced cooperation will henceforth be subject to the intergovernmental decision-making procedures provided for in the Treaties.
(2) The decision activating a bridging clause will stay in force for all legal acts that had been adopted within enhanced cooperation while it does not have any effect on other (new) legal acts adopted on the same legal basis. The existing legal acts could thus be amended or abrogated via the supranational procedures, while other acts would be subject to the intergovernmental procedures. One should keep mind that the bridging clause activated under enhanced

[17]Kuipers (2012), p. 216.

[18]European Parliament legislative resolution of 16 June 2010 on the draft Council decision authorising enhanced cooperation in the area of the law applicable to divorce and legal separation [2010/0066(NLE)], point 2.

[19]Admittedly, this is debated amongst European law scholars. While some authors reject the idea of an automatic transition into general Union law (see, for example, Zeitzmann (2015), p. 112), it seems that the majority tends towards an automatic transition (see, for example, Böttner (2016b), p. 537; Blanke, in Grabitz et al. (2016), Artikel 20 EUV, para 58; Lacchi (2013), p. 796).

cooperation can only apply to cases covered by the scope and objectives as specified in the authorising decision (Article 329 TFEU).

(3) The decision activating a bridging clause will—like all other legal acts—become part of the *acquis* without any exception so that the existing legal acts as well as any future legal acts will be subject to the supranational voting modalities. The bridging clause activated under Article 333 TFEU will thus have the same legal effects as a passerelle activated under Article 48(7) TEU. Again, however, it only applies to cases covered by the scope and objectives of the enhanced cooperation as approved by the authorising decision.

(4) The decision activating a bridging clause will become part of the *acquis* and henceforth apply to *all* legal acts adopted on the legal basis for which enhanced cooperation was used, even those exceeding the original scope and objectives of the cooperation.

The fourth alternative must be refused. It would mean that any act with a legal basis for which Article 333 TFEU has been activated, would be covered by the bridging clause, regardless of whether it falls within the scope of the enhanced cooperation approved under Article 329 TFEU. This would extend the effects of the enhanced cooperation beyond its material scope and thus run counter to the logic of that instrument.

By the same token, the first option is refused. All legal acts adopted within enhanced cooperation—including the bridging clauses—form a corpus of law specific to that cooperation. There is no basis on which the decision activating a bridging clause could be treated fundamentally differently. The first option outlined above would mean there is an automatic implicit revocation of the use of the bridging clause—without clear rational purpose.

On the other hand, the automatic transition of the use of the bridging clause adopted under the simpler procedure of Article 333 TFEU would circumvent and overturn the more rigid requirements stipulated under Article 48(7) TEU, namely the required consent of the European Parliament as well as the veto position of the national Parliaments. Frankly, one must admit that no other sector-specific bridging clause requires the consent of the European Parliament and only Article 81(3) TFEU includes a veto right for national Parliaments. However, these clauses are narrow in their scope of application whereas Article 48(7) TEU and Article 333 TFEU cover virtually all provisions and legal bases.

At least the problem of lack of national parliamentary veto is mitigated by the fact that participation in enhanced cooperation is fully voluntary, both before and after Article 333 TFEU is triggered. Furthermore, the national legislator can set up appropriate and even very strong parliamentary control mechanisms due to the requirement of unanimity (see Sect. 4.5 below). Consequently, there is no possibility that a Member State will be forced to accept a bridging clause or, conversely, will have no means to prevent the transition of a decision under Article 333 TFEU into the *acquis*. As a result, even though there is a certain degree of legal uncertainty from the wording of the Treaties, we favour the third interpretation outlined above, i.e. that a decision adopted under Article 333 TFEU will have the same effect as a decision adopted under Article 48(7) TEU once all Member States have acceded to an established enhanced cooperation. One should keep in mind, however, that this would cover future legal acts adopted on the basis affected by the bridging clause, but only insofar as they are falling within the scope of the original enhanced cooperation. As mentioned above (Sect. 2.3), a narrow definition of the scope of the bridging clause may lead to problems determining the applicable procedure for a legislative initiative.

3.3 Article 31(3) TEU as *Lex Specialis*?

A particularly interesting situation arises in the area of the Common Foreign and Security Policy.[20] The default voting requirement for this policy area, as Article 31 (1) TEU spells out, is unanimity in the Council, save as otherwise provided in the specific provisions. Apart from the exceptions to the unanimity laid down in Article 31(2) TEU, paragraph 3 of Article 31 TEU introduces a more general legal basis for the use of qualified majority voting: a decision by the European Council authorising action by qualified majority where unanimity would normally be required according to the Treaty. This opens the way to more cases of qualified majority voting in the Common Foreign and Security Policy without formal Treaty amendment. This new possibility of qualified majority voting potentially allows for an expedited process in the Council, once the European Council has agreed on it. It may be assumed that this situation relates to more structural issues, as the possibility to use qualified majority voting, once a Council decision is based on a decision by the European Council, is mentioned separately. This would mean that the European Council has been given the competence to extend the list of the four (current) exceptions to the unanimity rule as mentioned in Article 31(2) TEU.

The most important question regarding Article 31(3) TEU is its relationship to the general bridging clause of subparagraph 1 of Article 48(7) TEU, since only the latter—in conjunction with its third and fourth subparagraphs and Protocol No. 1—foresees participation of the European Parliament and of national parliaments in the application of the passerelle. In contrast, the wording of Article 31(3) TEU seems not to require the European Parliament's consent or grants a veto to the national Parliaments. Determining the relationship between these two provisions, however, is important, as both articles refer to one and the same area: Article 48(7)(1) of the TEU covers decisions in the TFEU as well as under Title V of the TEU (= Articles 21 through 46 TEU). On the other hand, paragraph 3 in conjunction with paragraphs 1 and 2 of Article 31 TEU refers to decisions under Chap. 2 of Title V of the TEU (= Articles 23 through 46 TEU). As Chap. 1 (Articles 21 and 22 TEU) does not contain any decision-making procedures, both bridging clauses cover the same field.

---

[20]See in more detail Böttner (2016a), p. 509 ff.

As both provisions are hierarchically and chronologically of the same status, the conflict-of-law rules of *lex superior derogat legi inferiori* (superior general norms prevail over inferior particular norms) and *lex posterior derogat legi priori* (later norms prevail over earlier norms) cannot be applied.[21] Only possible solution could thus be the *lex specialis* character of Article 31(3) TEU.

Under the Constitutional Treaty, the situation was quite clear. Article IV-444(1) of the Constitutional Treaty (which corresponds to the first subparagraph of Article 48(7) TEU) provided that where Part III (which contained the internal policies and the provisions on the Common Foreign and Security Policy) provides for the Council to act by unanimity in a given area or case, the European Council may adopt a European decision authorising the Council to act by a qualified majority in that area or in that case. Article III-300(3) contained the *passerelle* (now found in Article 31(3) TEU), *with the addition* that this decision shall be taken in accordance with Article I-40(7) of the Constitutional Treaty. This provision, entitled "Specific provisions relating to the common foreign and security policy" stipulated that the European Council may, unanimously, adopt a European decision authorising the Council to act by a qualified majority in cases other than those referred to in Part III. In this case, by way of reference in the relevant provisions and following the Treaty structure and systematics, Article III-300(3) of the Constitutional Treaty (now Article 31(3) TEU) was a true *lex specialis* to Article IV-444 (1) (now Article 48(7) TEU) of said Treaty. One could argue that it was the intention under the Treaty of Lisbon to preserve this situation and that the current situation is merely an editorial error. However, this error would be too gross and significant to be neglected.

Despite this, some argue that Article 31(3) TEU nonetheless still is *lex specialis* to Article 48(7) TEU, and thus prevails over the latter.[22] The German Federal Constitutional Court in its well-known judgment on the Treaty of Lisbon has, among others, also scrutinised the bridging clauses introduced with the Lisbon Treaty. The starting point of the Court's analysis is the "responsibility for integration" (*Integrationsverantwortung*), which means that in so far as the Member States elaborate treaty law in such a way as to allow treaty amendment without a national ratification procedure, whilst preserving the application of the principle of conferral, a special responsibility is incumbent on the legislative bodies, in addition to the Federal Government, within the context of participation which in Germany has to comply internally with the requirements under Article 23(1) of the Basic Law.[23] Any transfer of sovereign powers, including amendments of the Treaties

[21]Blanke, in Blanke and Mangiameli (2013), Article 1 TEU, para. 74.

[22]Some authors argue without further reasoning that Article 31(3) TEU is *lex specialis*. See Wessels and Bopp (2008), p. 24; Peers (2012), p. 65; Herrnfeld, in Schwarze (2012), Artikel 48 EUV, para. 18; Meng, in von der Groeben et al. (2015), Artikel 48 EUV, para. 24; Hummer, in Vedder and Heintschel von Heinegg (2012), Artikel 31 EUV, para. 10; Booß, in Lenz and Borchardt (2012), Artikel 48 EUV, para. 5. See also Wouters et al. (2008), p. 163.

[23]German Federal Constitutional Court, 2 BvE 2/08 and others, *Treaty of Lisbon*, judgment of 30 June 2009, ECLI:DE:BVerfG:2009:es20090630.2bve000208, headnote 2a.

which amend or supplement the content of the Basic Law or which make such amendments or supplements possible require the approval of two thirds of the members of the German *Bundestag* and two thirds of the votes of the *Bundesrat* (Article 23(1) third sentence in conjunction with Article 79(2) of the Basic Law).[24]

The transition from unanimity to qualified majority voting in the Council or from a special to the ordinary legislative procedure (which, in the majority of cases, also means that the Council decision is no longer adopted by unanimity but by a qualified majority) entail a loss of influence of the German representative in the Council as he will lose his veto power. As qualified majority voting in the Council and the ordinary legislative procedure are the normal procedures for law-making (Article 16(3) TEU, Article 289(1) in conjunction with Article 294 TFEU), the total extent to which the influence will be reduced by the introduction of qualified majority voting can at least be ascertained in a general manner.[25] However, the responsibility for integration requires that the loss of German influence in the Council which accompanies the exercise of the bridging clauses must be predictable also in individual cases at the time of the ratification of the Treaty of Lisbon by the German legislature in order for the approval given in advance by a Member State to a later treaty amendment is sufficiently democratically legitimised. The Court holds that the requirement of unanimity in the Council or the European Council for activating the bridging clauses is not sufficient because it may not always be sufficiently ascertainable for the national representatives to what extent the Member States' possibility of veto in the Council is thereby waived for future cases.[26] In the Court's view, the provisional safeguard under Article 48(7)(3) TEU is not a sufficient equivalent of the requirement of ratification and therefore the German legislative bodies can exercise their responsibility for integration in a given case and also decide whether the level of democratic legitimation is still high enough to accept the majority decision only if they pass a law within the meaning of Article 23(1) Basic Law.[27]

This holds true for the general bridging clauses of Article 48(7) TEU because, even though the cases of its application can be determined by the Treaties, the implications of its use from the point of view of national constitutional law are vast and hardly predictable. On the other hand, according to the Court, the special bridging clauses are limited to subject areas which are already sufficiently defined by the Treaty of Lisbon and therefore do not require a law within the meaning of Article 23(1) Basic Law. The Court names the special bridging clauses to which

---

[24]German Federal Constitutional Court, 2 BvR 2134, 2159/92, *Treaty of Maastricht*, judgment of 12 October 1993, BVerfGE 89, 155, p. 199, and 2 BvE 2/08 and others, *Treaty of Lisbon*, judgment of 30 June 2009, ECLI:DE:BVerfG:2009:es20090630.2bve000208, para. 312.

[25]German Federal Constitutional Court, 2 BvE 2/08 and others, *Treaty of Lisbon*, judgment of 30 June 2009, ECLI:DE:BVerfG:2009:es20090630.2bve000208, para. 317.

[26]German Federal Constitutional Court, 2 BvE 2/08 and others, *Treaty of Lisbon*, judgment of 30 June 2009, ECLI:DE:BVerfG:2009:es20090630.2bve000208, para. 318.

[27]German Federal Constitutional Court, 2 BvE 2/08 and others, *Treaty of Lisbon*, judgment of 30 June 2009, ECLI:DE:BVerfG:2009:es20090630.2bve000208, para. 319.

this line of argumentation applies; among them is Article 31(3) TEU.[28] Yet the Court does not provide any explanation as to why Article 31(3) TEU should be a true *lex specialis* to the general bridging clause. Apparently, it draws inspiration from the fact that Common Foreign and Security Policy, despite the abolishment of the pillar structure, is still a special area of competence.

Accordingly, in its effort to conform to the "responsibility for integration" that the Court regarded necessary, the German legislator has treated both provisions separately. The "Responsibility for Integration Act"[29] provides, in its Section 4(1), that the use of the general bridging clause (Article 48(7) TEU) requires a law pursuant to Article 23(1) of the Basic Law, whereas an Article 31(3) TEU decision merely requires approval by Parliament due to the provision's limited scope of application.

It appears that a number of authors have uncritically followed the German Constitutional Court and the German legislator in this assessment[30] while only a few give detailed explanations on their position. According to *Cremer*, Article 31(3) TEU only requires a unanimous European Council decision without further participation of other institutions. He holds that Article 31(3) TEU as *lex specialis* suppresses the application of Article 48(7) TEU for the Common Foreign and Security Policy, because this policy area, despite the supranational approaches, is still a mechanism for coordination of national foreign policy and thus it is not convincing to require parliamentary participation. This is justified by the European Parliament's limited role in Common Foreign and Security Policy (sentence 5 of the second subparagraph of Article 24(1) and Article 36 TEU). However, in his view, Article 48(7) TEU shall be applicable for Article 42(4) TEU in so far as decisions on Common Security and Defence Policy do not have military or defence implications and for Article 41 TEU on the financing of the Common Foreign and Security Policy. This is based on the grounds that according to Article 31(1) TEU decisions under that Chapter shall be taken by the European Council and the Council acting unanimously, *except where this Chapter provides otherwise*, and the aforementioned provisions contain rules on Council votes. Moreover, in his view, participation of the parliaments in accordance with Article 48(7) is justified for Article 41 TEU as changes to decision-making in the budgetary law require consent of the majority of the Members of the European Parliament. However, *Cremer* admits that this construction is not very consistent and rather unfortunate as it would be detrimental to the intended enhancement of democratic legitimation of the

---

[28]German Federal Constitutional Court, 2 BvE 2/08 and others, *Treaty of Lisbon*, judgment of 30 June 2009, ECLI:DE:BVerfG:2009:es20090630.2bve000208, para. 320 f.

[29]Act on the Exercise by the Bundestag and by the Bundesrat of their Responsibility for Integration in Matters concerning the European Union (Responsibility for Integration Act) of 22 September 2009, as amended by Article 1 of the Act of 1 December 2009.l.

[30]Ohler, in Grabitz et al. (2011), Artikel 48 EUV, para. 54; Kaufmann-Bühler, in Grabitz et al. (2011), Artikel 42 EUV, para. 74 and 77; Regelsberger and Kugelmann, Streinz (2012), Artikel 31 EUV, para 14.

Union by the Treaty of Lisbon, especially with regard to national parliaments (Article 2, Article 10, Article 12(d) TEU).[31]

In fact, even though the Treaty of Lisbon has formally abolished the former pillar structure of the EC/EU, the Common Foreign and Security Policy maintains a peculiar nature that is different from the supranational policies and remains a *sui generis* category of competence.[32] Due to its special nature, the Common Foreign and Security Policy is subject to specific rules and procedures. According to Articles 24(1) and 31(1) of the TEU this includes unanimity in the Council as *lex specialis* to the default voting rule of qualified majority (Article 16(3) TEU),[33] the exclusion of legislative acts[34] and specific roles for the European Parliament, the Commission and the Court of Justice of the European Union.[35] *P. van Elsuwege*: points out "the executive dominance over foreign affairs, as it exists in the constitutional traditions of many countries in the world. [...] The strategic character of foreign policy and the inherent importance of confidentiality and flexibility in its decision-making all explain why this area is considered a prerogative of the executive power."[36]

It is held that, due to the specific nature of Common Foreign and Security Policy, participation of the European Parliament—especially due to its limited role as indicated by sentence 5 of the second subparagraph of Article 24(1) TEU[37]—and of national parliaments contradicts the (still) executive and intergovernmental character of Common Foreign and Security Policy. Under this interpretation, notifying the European Parliament (Article 36 TEU) would suffice. In this context, Declaration No. 14 states that provisions concerning Common Foreign and Security Policy shall not increase the role of the European Parliament. Systematic reasons and the *telos* of the voting rules in Common Foreign and Security Policy could therefore justify the application of Article 31(3) instead of Article 48(7) TEU as *passerelle* in the area of Common Foreign and Security Policy. In that respect, Article 31(3) TEU could be one of the "specific rules and procedures" mentioned in Article 24(1) TEU for the Common Foreign and Security Policy.

However, the *lex specialis* argument is rather weak and the mentioning of any "rules and procedures" that are "specific" to the still intergovernmentally designed area of foreign policy does not necessarily mean that *all* rules and procedures are of a particular nature. This finding is not contradicted by the "membrane" between the

---

[31] Cremer, in Calliess and Ruffert (2016), Artikel 31 EUV, para. 18, and Artikel 48 EUV, para. 16.

[32] Orzan, in Curti Gialdino (2012), Articolo 31 TUE, p. 331 (333).

[33] On unanimity voting in international organisations in general, see Böttner and Wessel, in Blanke and Mangiameli (2013), Article 31 TEU, para. 7.

[34] Terpan, in Blanke and Mangiameli (2013), Article 24 TEU, para 16 ff.; Böttner and Wessel, in Blanke and Mangiameli (2013), Article 31 TEU, para. 13–15.

[35] See on this also Eeckhout (2012), p. 279 ff.

[36] van Elsuwege (2011), p. 999. See also Kaufmann-Bühler and Meyer-Landrut, in Grabitz et al. (2010), Artikel 31 EUV, para 10.

[37] Terpan, in Blanke and Mangiameli (2013), Article 24 TEU, para. 20.

supranational policies and Common Foreign and Security Policy as laid down in Article 40 TEU, as it simply states that the implementation of either policy shall not affect the other; it does not say anything about a complete separation between these two areas and procedural issues may apply for both areas (e.g. the qualified majority as defined in Article 16(3) TEU, which applies to both supranational policy and Common Foreign and Security Policy).

On the other hand, the extension of qualified majority voting (Article 31(2) TEU;[38] as long as these decisions do not have military or defence implications, Article 31(4) TEU[39]) and the possibility of constructive abstention[40] indicate that Common Foreign and Security since Amsterdam is no longer a purely intergovernmental area.[41] Furthermore, both Article 31 and Article 48 TEU expressly provide for their application to the area of Common Foreign and Security Policy. The duplication of the *passerelle* clauses could thus be justified with systematic reasons and with the concept of the "unity of the constitution": Article 48 TEU lists the Treaty revisions procedures. In order to give an exhaustive list in one place/ provision, this Article also lists the *passerelle* clause for the Common Foreign and Security Policy. Article 31 TEU on the other hand lists the voting procedures and especially the application of qualified majority voting within Common Foreign and Security Policy. The list in Article 31 TEU would be incomplete without at least giving a "reminder" to the bridging clause, which is also applicable to these provisions. Thus, Article 31(3) TEU needs to be read and applied *in combination* with Article 48(7) TEU.[42] Article 48(7) TEU supplements Article 31(3) TEU in that it lays down the procedure to be followed,[43] including the veto right of national

[38]See in detail Böttner and Wessel, in Blanke and Mangiameli (2013), Article 31 TEU, para. 32–35. Qualified majority voting is also possible in a limited number of other cases, e.g. the establishment and financing of a start-up fund for military and defence operations (Article 41(3)(3) TEU), the establishment of the European Defence Agency (Article 45(2) TEU) and some decisions in relation to the Permanent Structured Cooperation (Article 46 TEU) in the Common Security and Defence Policy. As a counter-weight to these exceptions, the Treaty maintained the 'emergency brake' (as a codification of the 1966 Luxembourg Compromise) for situations in which a member of the Council declares that, for vital and stated reasons of national policy, it intends to oppose the adoption of a decision to be taken by qualified majority voting (see Böttner and Wessel, in Blanke and Mangiameli (2013), Article 31 TEU, para. 38–41).

[39]Böttner and Wessel, in Blanke and Mangiameli (2013), Article 31 TEU, para. 50–53.

[40]See Böttner and Wessel, in Blanke and Mangiameli (2013), Article 31 TEU, para. 16 ff.

[41]Cf. Marquardt and Gaedtke, in von der Groeben et al. (2015), Artikel 31 EUV, para. 2.

[42]For an application of Article 48(7) TEU also Regelsberger (2008), p. 273; Marquardt and Gaedtke, in von der Groeben et al. (2015), Artikel 31 EUV, para. 12. Unclear Rathke, in von Arnauld and Hufeld (2010), IntVG, para. 81 (combination of the special bridging clauses and Article 48(7) TEU) and para. 97 (national parliaments have no veto under Article 31 TEU).

[43]With the same view Schmalenbach, in Mayer and Stöger (2013), Artikel 31 EUV, para. 26; see also Lang, in Pocar and Baruffi (2014), Articolo 31 TUE, para. 4. Kaufmann-Bühler and Meyer-Landrut, in Grabitz et al. (2010), Artikel 31 EUV, para. 37, base the application of Article 48(7) TEU on the fact that Article 31(3) TEU does not give any further indications regarding the procedure for the use of the *passerelle* clause.

parliaments and the necessary consent of the European Parliament. Taking into account the peculiarities of Common Foreign and Security Policy, it seems valid to confer the power to initiate a decision under Article 31(3) TEU to the High Representative, who shall contribute by his proposals to the development of the Common Foreign and Security Policy (Article 18(2) and Article 27(1) TEU).[44]

In fact, the exclusion of legislative acts primarily has to do with the exclusion of the legislative *procedure* (Article 289(3) TFEU) and hence with the inapplicability of the role of the Commission and the European Parliament in this procedure (Article 24(1)(2), sentence 5, TEU)[45] as well as with the limited role of the Court of Justice in deciding on the legality or the interpretation of a Common Foreign and Security Policy act (cf. Article 24(1)(2), sentence 6 TEU)[46]. However, while the European Parliament is not involved in the decision making in Common Foreign and Security Policy, i.e. in the adoption of legal acts that produce effects vis-à-vis third parties and that determine the Union's external action, this does not necessarily mean that Parliament should be excluded from decisions on procedural rules. The rules on Common Foreign and Security Policy therefore do not preclude Parliament from being involved in the decision to make use of the *passerelle* under Article 31(3) TEU. Likewise, the Court, while not having jurisdiction over most of the substantive Common Foreign and Security Policy acts, is not barred from reviewing decisions with regard to their formal legality, including decisions on the bridging procedure. As the Czech Constitutional Court correctly points out, such decisions are "reviewable by the Court of Justice as regards their consistency with the Treaty itself, which proves that they are not amendments to the Treaties, but, on the contrary, the Treaties retain a higher legal force over these acts […] and so these acts must be consistent with the conditions that the Treaties set out for them".[47]

Furthermore, both Articles 48(7) and Article 31(3) TEU lead to changes in the primary law of the Union (the Treaties).[48] With regard to more democratic legitimation of Union action in connection with a more supranational approach, even in Common Foreign and Security Policy matters after the Treaty of Lisbon, full application of the procedure foreseen in Article 48(7) TEU is justified. In this context, it needs to be recalled that democracy is one of the fundamental values of the EU, as mentioned in Article 2 TEU, which also applies to the Union's external action (see Articles 21 and 22 TEU). The involvement of national parliaments and the European Parliament, however, may constitute an insurmountable obstacle in practice, leaving this passerelle unimplemented.

---

[44] Kaufmann-Bühler and Meyer-Landrut, in Grabitz et al. (2010), Artikel 31 EUV, para. 37.

[45] Terpan, in Blanke and Mangiameli (2013), Article 24 TEU, para. 19–21.

[46] Terpan, in Blanke and Mangiameli (2013), Article 24 TEU, para. 22.

[47] Czech Constitutional Court, Pl. US 19/08, *Treaty of Lisbon I*, decision of 26 November 2008, ECLI:CZ:US:2008:Pl.US.19.08.1, para. 162 f.

[48] Rathke, in von Arnauld and Hufeld (2010), IntVG, para. 92.

3.4 "Semi-Passerelle" Clauses

For the sake of completeness, a few remarks are necessary on two provisions that one could call "semi-passerelles" or "small *Kompetenz-Kompetenz*".[49] These are Article 82(2)(d) and Article 83(1)(3) of the TFEU, both in the area of judicial cooperation in criminal matters.

According to Article 82(2) TFEU, in order to facilitate mutual recognition of judgments and judicial decisions and police and judicial cooperation in criminal matters having a cross-border dimension, the European Parliament and the Council may establish minimum rules by means of directives adopted through the ordinary legislative procedure. Subparagraphs (a) through (c) lists certain areas for which this shall apply, namely mutual admissibility of evidence between Member States, the rights of individuals in criminal procedure and the rights of victims of crime. Subparagraph d), in addition, allows for the adoption of minimum rules on "any other specific aspects of criminal procedure" which has been identified by the Council by unanimous decision and with the consent of the European Parliament.

In a similar manner, Article 83(1) TFEU provides that the European Parliament and the Council may, by means of directives adopted in accordance with the ordinary legislative procedure, establish minimum rules concerning the definition of criminal offences and sanctions in the areas of particularly serious crime with a cross-border dimension resulting from the nature or impact of such offences or from a special need to combat them on a common basis. The provision goes on and names these areas of crime: terrorism, trafficking in human beings and sexual exploitation of women and children, illicit drug trafficking, illicit arms trafficking, money laundering, corruption, counterfeiting of means of payment, computer crime and organised crime. On the basis of subparagraph 3 of Article 83(1) TFEU, the Council, by unanimous vote and with the consent of the European Parliament, may adopt a decision identifying other areas of crime that meet the criteria specified in that paragraph.

Both provisions are a form of simplified treaty revision, as they lead to amendments in primary law. Unlike the passerelle clauses, however, they do not do so by shifting from existing intergovernmental to supranational voting and decision-making procedures. Nevertheless, they closely resemble the bridging clauses in that by means of a unanimous Council decision and with the consent of the European Parliament, specific (newly added) aspects or areas will be subject to the ordinary legislative procedure. Of course, the requirement for a unanimous Council decision could itself be replaced by qualified majority voting *pro futuro* by the general passerelle of Article 48(7) TEU.

---

[49]With this wording Vogel and Eisele, in Grabitz et al. (2015), Artikel 82 AEUV, para. 111.

The German term "Kompetenz-Kompetenz" describes the power to decide on one's own competences. The European Union does not dispose of this power, but instead is subject to the conferral of competences (Article 5(2) TEU).

References

Becker U (1998) Differenzierung der Rechtseinheit durch "abgestufte Integration". Europarecht Beiheft 1/1998, 29–57

Blanke H-J, Mangiameli S (eds) (2013) The treaty on European Union—a commentary. Springer, Heidelberg

Böttner R (2016a) The Treaty amendment procedures and the relationship between Article 31(3) TEU and the general bridging clause of Article 48(7) TEU. Eur Const Law Rev 499–521

Böttner R (2016b) Eine Idee lernt laufen—zur Praxis der Verstärkten Zusammenarbeit nach Lissabon. Zeitschrift für europarechtliche Studien 501–549

Böttner R (2017) Brückenklauseln im europäischen Verfassungsrecht. Europarecht 381–401

Calliess C, Ruffert M (eds) (2016) EUV/AEUV, 5th edn. C.H.Beck, Munich

Curti Gialdino C (ed) (2012) Codice dell'Unione europea operativo. TUE e TFUE commentati articolo per articolo. Simone, Naples

Eeckhout P (2012) The EU's common foreign and security policy after Lisbon. In: Biondi A, Eeckhout P, Ripley S (eds) EU law after Lisbon. Oxford University Press, Oxford, pp 265–291

Geiger R, Khan D-E, Kotzur M (eds) (2017) EUV/AEUV, 6th edn. C.H.Beck, Munich

Grabitz E, Hilf M, Nettesheim M (eds) (2009 ff.) Das Recht der Europäischen Union: EUV/AEUV. loose leaf. C.H.Beck, Munich

Kuipers JJ (2012) The law applicable to divorce as test ground for enhanced cooperation. Eur Law J 201–229

Lacchi C (2013) Développements récents sur les coopérations renforcées. Revue des affaires européennes 785–801

Lenz C-O, Borchardt KD (eds) (2012) EU-Verträge, Kommentar. Bundesanzeiger Verlag, Bonn

Mayer H, Stöger K (eds) (2013) Kommentar zu EUV und AEUV. Manz, Vienna

Peers S (2012) The future of EU treaty amendments. Yearb Eur Law 17–111

Pocar F, Baruffi MC (eds) (2014) Commentario Breve ai Trattati dell'Unione Europea, 2nd edn. Cedam, Padova

Regelsberger E (2008) Von Nizza nach Lissabon—das neue konstitutionelle Angebot für die Gemeinsame Außen- und Sicherheitspolitik der EU. Integration 266–281

Reimer F (2016) Juristische Methodenlehre. Nomos, Baden-Baden

Schwarze J (ed) (2012) EU-Verträge, 3rd edn. Nomos, Baden-Baden

Streinz R (ed) (2012) EUV/AEUV, 2nd edn. C.H.Beck, Munich

van Elsuwege P (2011) EU external action after the collapse of the pillar structure: in search of a new balance between delimitation and consistency. Common Market Law Rev 987–1019

Vedder C, Heintschel von Heinegg W (eds) (2012) Europäisches Unionsrecht: EUV, AEUV, Grundrechte-Charta; Handkommentar. Nomos, Baden-Baden

von Arnauld A, Hufeld U (eds) (2010) Systematischer Kommentar zu den Lissabon-Begleitgesetzen. Nomos, Baden-Baden

von der Groeben H, Schwarze J, Hatje A (eds) (2015) Europäisches Unionsrecht, 7th edn. Nomos, Baden-Baden

Wessels W, Bopp F (2008) The institutional architecture of common foreign and security policy after the Lisbon Treaty—Constitutional breakthrough or challenges ahead? CHALLENGE Research Paper No. 10

Wouters J, Coppens D, De Meester B (2008) The European Union's external relations after the Lisbon Treaty. In: Griller S, Ziller J (eds) The Lisbon Treaty. EU Constitutionalism without a Constitutional Treaty? Heidelberg, Springer, pp 143–204

Zeitzmann S (2015) Zu viel gewollt, zu wenig geregelt? Das komplizierte Verhältnis der Verstärkten Zusammenarbeit zum acquis communautaire. In: Stratenschulte E (ed) Der Anfang vom Ende? Formen differenzierter Integration und ihre Konsequenzen. Baden-Baden, Nomos, pp 103–134

Chapter 4
Procedure for Activating the General Bridging Clauses

No matter which of the general bridging clauses is to be activated, subparagraphs 3 and 4 of Article 48(7) TEU provide for a uniform procedure. The right of initiative belongs to the European Council (Sect. 4.2). Any national Parliament can veto the initative (Sect. 4.3). The national Parliaments are thus for the first time *directly* included in the European decision-making procedures.[1] Furthermore, the European Parliament has to give its consent (Sect. 4.4). Only then can the European Council adopt the decision (Sect. 4.5). In the end of this section, we shortly discuss to what extent the rules and interpretations regarding the procedures for activating the general bridging clauses are applicable or relevant for the special bridging clauses (Sect. 4.6). This Chapter includes also an overview over the national Parliaments (Table 4.1) as well as an overview over the most important legal acts regarding their involvement in the activation of the bridging clauses (Table 4.2).

4.1 Participation of the National Parliaments in General

The most complicated aspect of the procedure is the participation of national Parliaments, which may have different forms and manifest itself in different phases of the procedure:

- veto power of the national Parliament according to Article 48(7) TEU (Sect. 4.3);
- previous parliamentary consent required under the national law for the positive vote of the representative in the European Council on the adoption of the decision of the European Council (Sect. 4.5);
- general parliamentary control powers in EU affairs that can be exercised towards the representative in the European Council before the European Council initiates

[1]Mayer (2012), p. 89 f.

R. Böttner and J. Grinc, *Bridging Clauses in European Constitutional Law*, SpringerBriefs in Law, https://doi.org/10.1007/978-3-319-73341-8_4

Table 4.1 National parliaments of EU Member States

Member state	Legislative Assembly	
	Lower house	Upper house
Austria	Austrian Parliament (*Österreichisches Parlament*), [Federal Assembly (*Bundesversammlung*)]	
	National Council (*Nationalrat*)	Federal Council (*Bundesrat*)
Belgium[a]	Federal Parliament (*Federaal Parlement/Parlement Fédéral/Föderales Parlament*)	
	Chamber of Representatives (*Kamer van Volksvertegenwoordigers/Chambre des Représentants/Abgeordnetenkammer*)	Senate (*Senaat/Sénat/ Senat*)
Bulgaria	National Assembly (*Народно събрание*)	
Croatia	Croatian Parliament (*Hrvatski Sabor*)	
Cyprus	House of Representatives (*Βουλή των Αντιπροσώπων/Temsilciler Meclisi*)	
Czech Republic	Chamber of Deputies (*Poslanecká sněmovna*)	Senate (*Senát*)
Denmark	Parliament (*Folketing*)	
Estonia	State Assembly (*Riigikogu*)	
Finland	Parliament (*Eduskunta/Riksdag*)	
France	Parliament (*Parlement*) [Congress (*Congrès*)]	
	National Assembly (*Assemblée nationale*)	Senate (*Sénat*)
Germany	Federal Diet (*Bundestag*)	Federal Council (*Bundesrat*)
	[Federal Assembly (*Bundesversammlung*)][b]	
Greece	Assembly of the Greeks (*Βουλή των Ελλήνων*)	
Hungary	National Assembly (*Országgyűlés*)	
Ireland	Parliament (*Oireachtas*)	
	House of Representatives (*Dáil Éireann*)	Senate (*Seanad Éireann*)
Italy	Parliament (*Parlamento*)	
	Chamber of Deputies (*Camera dei Deputati*)	Senate of the Republic (*Senato della Repubblica*)
Latvia	Diet (*Saeima*)	
Lithuania	Diet (*Seimas*)	
Luxembourg	Chamber of Deputies (*Chambre des Députés/Abgeordnetenkammer/Châmber vun Députéirten*)	
Malta	Chamber of Deputies (*Kamra tad-Deputati*)	
Netherlands	States-General (*Staten–Generaal*)	
	Second Chamber/House of Representatives (*Tweede Kamer*)	First Chamber/Senate (*Eerste Kamer*)

(Continued)

Table 4.1 (Continued)

Member state	Legislative Assembly	
	Lower house	Upper house
Poland	National Assembly (*Zgromadzenie Narodowe*)	
	Diet (*Sejm*)	Senate (*Senat*)
Portugal	Assembly of the Republic (*Assembleia da República*)	
Romania	Parliament (*Parlamentul*)	
	Chamber of Deputies (*Camera Deputaţilor*)	Senate (*Senat*)
Slovakia	National Council (*Národná rada*)	
Slovenia	Parliament (*Parlament*)	
	National Assembly (*Državni zbor*)	National Council (*Državni svet*)
Spain	General Courts (*Cortes Generales*)	
	Congress of Deputies (*Congreso de los Diputados*)	Senate (*Senado*)
Sweden	Diet (*Riksdag*)	
United Kingdom	Parliament	
	House of Commons	House of Lords
Bicameral national Parliaments		

[a]Due to the complex constitutional system, also the parliamentary assemblies of the Communities and the Regions act as components of the national parliamentary system or chambers of the national Parliament (cf. Declaration No. 51 annexed to the Treaties). These are: the Brussels Regional Parliament (*Brussels Hoofdstedelijk Parlement/Parlement de la Région de Bruxelles-Capitale*), the Flemish Parliament (*Vlaams Parlement*), the Walloon Parliament (*Parlement wallon*), the Parliament of the French Community (*Parlement de la Communauté française*) and the Parliament of the German-speaking Community (*Parlament der Deutschsprachigen Gemeinschaft*)
[b]The Federal Assembly is not the joint legislature, but a convention of the Federal Diet, the Federal Council and other members for the purpose of electing the Federal President

the procedure (Sect. 4.1) or before the decision is adopted by the European Council (Sect. 4.5).

By granting each national Parliament the right to veto a decision agreed upon by their Head of State or Government, the EU law touches upon the executive–parliamentary relations in the constitutional law of the Member States. This leads to a number of questions.

First, there are Member States that are represented in the European Council by their Head of State (president) rather than by the Head of Government (federal chancellor, prime minister). It is usual in the EU Member States, most of which count among parliamentary forms of government, that the Head of State is not politically accountable to the parliament, or at least not in the same way as the government (i.e. through a majority vote of no confidence). All Heads of State currently attending the European Council are directly elected presidents. This

Table 4.2 Sources of relevant national law applicable to the participation of the national Parliaments in the procedures for the activation of the bridging clauses

Austria	Federal Constitutional Law of 20 October 1920, as amended
Bulgaria	Rules of Procedure of the National Assembly, Prom. SG. No. 35 of 2 May 2017 (http://www.parliament.bg/en/rulesoftheorganisations)
Croatia	Act on the Co-Operation of the Croatian Parliament and the Government of the Republic of Croatia in European Affairs, NN 81/13 (http://www.sabor.hr/act-on-the-co-operation-of-the-croatian-parliame01)
Cyprus	Constitution of Cyprus from 16 August 1960, as amended
Czech Republic	1. Constitutional Act No. 1/1993 Coll., Constitution of the Czech Republic, as amended 2. Act No. 90/1995 Coll., on the Rules of Procedure of the Chamber of Deputies (as amended) (http://www.psp.cz/en/docs/laws/1995/90.html) 3. Act No. 107/1999 Coll, on the Standing Rules of the Senate (as amended) (http://www.senat.cz/informace/zakon106/zakony/zak107-eng.php?ke_dni=10.11.2017&O=11)
Denmark	1. Constitutional Act of Denmark of 5 June 1953, as amended 2. Act No. 321 of 30 April 2008 on the Ratification of the Lisbon Treaty amending the Act No. 447 of 11 October 1972 on the Accession of Denmark to the European Communities, as amended (https://www.retsinformation.dk/Forms/R0710.aspx?id=116752) 3. Standing Orders of the Danish Parliament (http://www.thedanishparliament.dk/publications/standing%20orders%20of%20the%20folketing.aspx?page=all)
Estonia	Riigikogu Rules of Procedure and Internal Rules Act (RT I 2007, 44, 316), as amended (https://www.riigiteataja.ee/en/eli/518112014003/consolide)
Finland	Parliament's Rules of Procedure from 17 December 1999 (40/2000), as amended (https://www.eduskunta.fi/EN/tietoaeduskunnasta/Documents/RulesofProcedure_20150416.pdf)
France	1. Constitution of 4 October 1958, as amended 2. Rules of Procedure of the National Assembly (http://www2.assemblee-nationale.fr/langues/welcome-to-the-english-website-of-the-french-national-assembly) 3. Standing Orders of the Senate (http://www.senat.fr/fileadmin/Fichiers/Images/lng/Standing_orders_of_the_Senate.pdf)
Germany	1. Basic Law for the Federal Republic of Germany, as amended 2. Act on Cooperation between the Federal Government and the German Bundestag in Matters concerning the European Union of 4 July 2013 (Federal Law Gazette [BGBl.] Part I p. 2170) (http://www.gesetze-im-internet.de/englisch_euzbbg/englisch_euzbbg.html) 3. Act on the Exercise by the Bundestag and by the Bundesrat of their Responsibility for Integration in Matters concerning the European Union (Responsibility for Integration Act) from the Federal Republic of Germany of 22 September 2009 (Federal Law Gazette I, p. 3022), last amended by Article 1 of the Act of 1 December 2009 (Federal Law Gazette I, p. 3822) (https://www.gesetze-im-internet.de/englisch_intvg/englisch_intvg.html)
Greece	Standing Orders of the Parliament, Government Gazette No. 106 A'/24.6.1987, as amended (http://www.hellenicparliament.gr/en/Vouli-ton-Ellinon/Kanonismos-tis-Voulis/)

(continued)

Table 4.2 (continued)

Hungary	1. Act XXXVI/2012 on the National Assembly, as amended (http://www.parlament.hu/documents/125505/138409/Act+XXXVI+of+2012+on+the+National+Assembly/b53726b7-12a8-4d93-acef-140feef44395) 2. Resolution 10/2014. (II. 24.) OGY on certain provisions of the Rules of Procedure (http://www.parlament.hu/documents/125505/138409/Resolution+on+certain+provisions+of+the+Rules+of+Procedure/968f2e08-f740-4241-a87b-28e6dc390407)
Ireland	1. Constitution of Ireland of 1 July 1937, as amended 2. European Union Act 2009, No. 33 from 27 October 2009 (http://www.irishstatutebook.ie/eli/2009/act/33/enacted/en/html) 3. European Communities (Amendment) Act 2012, No. 21 of 3 July 2012 (http://www.irishstatutebook.ie/eli/2012/act/21/enacted/en/pdf) 4. Standing Orders of Dáil (2016) (http://www.oireachtas.ie/parliament/media/about/standingorders/Standing-Orders-2016.pdf) 5. Standing Orders of the Seanad (2017) (http://www.oireachtas.ie/parliament/media/about/standingorders/Seanad-Standing-Orders-2017.pdf)
Italy	Law No. 234/2012 of 24 December 2012 on general rules on Italy's participation in formation and implementation of EU legislation and policies (Official Gazette No. 3 from 4 January 2013) (http://www.gazzettaufficiale.it/eli/id/2013/01/04/13G00003/sg)
Lithuania	1. Constitution of the Republic of Lithuania of 25 October 1992, as amended 2. Constitutional Act on Membership of the Republic of Lithuania in the European Union (No. IX-2343) of 13 July 2004, Valstybės žinios (Official Gazette), 2004, No. 111–4123 (https://e-seimas.lrs.lt/portal/legalAct/lt/TAD/TAIS.239806?jfwid=-9dzqnu3dq) 3. Statute of the Seimas of the Republic of Lithuania, 17 February 1994 No I-399, as last amended on 22 December 2015—No. XII-2211 (https://e-seimas.lrs.lt/portal/legalAct/lt/TAD/e495a6e2b60611e5be9bf78e07ed6470?jfwid=-fxdp70yw)
Malta	Act to provide for Malta's accession to the European Union and to make provision consequent and ancillary thereto (European Union Act), Act V of 2003, as amended by Act III of 2006, Legal Notice 427 of 2007 and Act VII of 2012. (http://www.justiceservices.gov.mt/DownloadDocument.aspx?app=lom&itemid=8926&l=1)
Poland	1. Act of 8 October 2010 on the cooperation of the Council of Ministers with the Sejm and the Senate in matters relating to the Republic of Poland's membership of the European Union, as published in Dziennik Ustaw of 2010, No. 213, item 1395 (http://www.sejm.gov.pl/prawo/ustawa_kooperacyjna_eng/kon12.htm) 2. Standing Orders of the Sejm of the Republic of Poland, Resolution of 30 July 1992, as published in Monitor Polski, item 32 and as further amended 3. Rules and Regulations of the Senate; Resolution of the Senate of the Republic of Poland of November 23, 1990, as published in Monitor Polski of 2015, item 805 and as further amended (http://www.senat.gov.pl/en/about-the-senate/regulamin-senatu/)

(continued)

Table 4.2 (continued)

Romania	1. Constitution of Romania of 1991, as republished in the Official Gazette of Romania, Part I, No. 758 of 29 October 2003 and as amended 2. Act No. 373/2013 on cooperation between the Parliament and the Government in the field of European affairs (http://www.cdep.ro/pdfs/LG_373_2013.pdf)
Slovakia	Constitutional Act No. 397/2004 Coll. on the cooperation between the National Council of the Slovak Republic and the Government of the Slovak Republic in matters concerning the European Union. (http://www.ipex.eu/IPEXL-WEB/dossier/files/download/082dbcc5517ee420015181232061 0174.do)
Slovenia	1. Constitution of the Republic of Slovenia, Official Gazette of the Republic of Slovenia Nos. 33/91-I, 42/97, 66/2000, 24/03, 69/04, 68/06, and 47/13 2. Act on Cooperation between the National Assembly and the Government in EU affairs (http://imss.dz-rs.si/imis/22c409026235aa98a901.pdf) 3. Rules of Procedure of the National Assembly of 2 April 2002 (PoDZ-1—Official Gazette of the Republic of Slovenia No. 35/02), as amended (http://imss.dz-rs.si/imis/7f209c2691236403aa9b.pdf)
Spain	1. Law 8/1994, of 19 May, regulating the Joint Parliamentary European Union Committee, as amended by Law 24/2009 (http://www.boe.es/buscar/act.php?id=BOE-A-1994-11418) 2. Resolution of the Bureaus of the Congress of Deputies and the Senate, 21 September 1995, developing Law 8/1994, of 19 May, regulating the Joint Parliamentary European Union Committee
Sweden	Riksdag Act (2014:801), as amended (https://www.riksdagen.se/globalassets/07.-dokument–lagar/the-riksdag-act-2015.pdf)
United Kingdom	European Union Act 2011 (2011, Chapter 12) (https://www.legislation.gov.uk/ukpga/2011/12/pdfs/ukpga_20110012_en.pdf)

concerns Cyprus,[2] which has a presidential form of government where the functions of the Head of State and the Head of Government are combined in the office of the President, and France,[3] Lithuania[4] and Romania.[5] In the latter three Member States, which are usually considered to be semi-presidential systems,[6] the division of powers between the president and the government (and prime minister) in the area of external relations and especially in EU affairs and representation of the state in

[2]Article 39(1) of the Constitution; see on this Zervakis and Costeas (2010), p. 1105 f.; Markides (2014), p. 277 ff.

[3]Articles 5, 6(1), 20 and 52 of the Constitution; see on this Kempf (2009), p. 356; Kortmann (2014), p. 581 ff.

[4]Articles 78(2) and 84(1) of the Constitution; see on this Tauber (2010), p. 176 f.; Vaičaitis (2014), p. 1043 ff.

[5]Articles 80, 81(1) and 91 of the Constitution; see on this Gabanyi (2010), p. 636 f.; Ionescu (2014), p. 1372 ff.

[6]See e.g. Elgie (1999).

the European Council is blurred and is rather a matter of constitutional and political practice than of precise delimitation in the constitution itself.[7]

The question is how parliamentary participation, especially the EU law based veto power, fits in with national systems where the representative in the European Council is not politically accountable to the parliament. Here, the Treaty-amending character of the bridging clauses must be borne in mind. Ratification of most important international agreements requires parliamentary participation in all EU Member States. The veto power of the national Parliaments under Article 48(7) TEU reflects this. Furthermore, the constitutional law of the respective states does not necessarily preclude the other forms of parliamentary participation. In Cyprus and France, where the dominant role of the president is perhaps most strongly established, we find no formal procedure for parliamentary decision-making on the president's mandate for the European Council meetings. But the situation is different in Romania (despite the obvious inspiration by the French system), where the Government has to present to the Parliament the proposed mandate for the meeting of the European Council and the Parliament may "adopt proposals concerning the mandate" that shall be "taken into account in the mandate drafted by the Government".[8] In Lithuania, the Statute of the Seimas includes European Council meetings in the mandating procedures and reporting duties of the Government, suggesting a shared responsibility of the Head of State, government and parliament in EU affairs.[9]

Second, it has been argued that Article 48(7) TEU regulates the participation of national Parliaments in the general bridging clause procedure exclusively and exhaustively, leaving no space for additional national procedures. In other words, the veto power is viewed as the sole form of participation of national Parliaments in the bridging clause procedure defined and sanctioned by EU law. The national law based requirement of previous parliamentary consent with the adoption of the decision in the European Council (Sect. 4.5) is considered to be contrary to EU law. The argument is supported by the distinctions EU law makes between various treaty-amending procedures: ratification in the ordinary revision procedure, "approval by the Member States in accordance with their respective constitutional

[7]Of course, there are other Member States with directly elected Heads of State, such as Poland or Bulgaria, but where the leading role in the EU policy clearly remains with the government accountable to the parliament. In Poland, the Constitutional Tribunal had to interpret that it is primarily the Prime Minister and not the President who represents the state in the European Council (Ref. No. Kpt 2/08, decision of 20 May 2009). The subsequently adopted Act of 8 October 2010 on the cooperation of the Council of Ministers with the Sejm and the Senate in matters relating to the Republic of Poland's membership of the European Union provides that it is the President who decides on the position of the Republic of Poland in relation to the bridging clauses. However, the President acts on proposal of the Council of Ministers and with consent granted by a statute. See Sections 14 and 15 of the aforementioned act.

[8]Article 18 of the Act No. 373/2013 on cooperation between the Parliament and the Government in the field of European affairs.

[9]Cf. Articles 180^9 and 180^{17} of the Statute of the Seimas; see also Vilpišauskas (2015), pp. 563–569.

requirements" in the simplified revision procedure and in other cases, and, finally, the veto power regarding the general bridging clauses and the special bridging clause of Article 81(3) second and third subparagraph TFEU.[10]

In our opinion, this view disregards the role of national Parliaments both in the European and in the national context as well as the constitutional structure of the Member States. The second subparagraph of Article 10(2) TEU acknowledges the democratic accountability and therefore also the parliamentary control over the actions of Member States' representatives in the European Council and Council, which may have different intensity and legal effects in different Member States. The requirement of previous parliamentary consent in certain Member States is an element of the will formation of the Member State, not a modification of the EU law-based parliamentary veto procedure (which actually also provides a safeguard in case of an *ultra vires* action of the representative in the European Council). If the parliamentary veto were to be considered the only way the national Parliament can bind the national European Council representative regarding the Article 48(7) TEU procedure without violating EU law, it would mean that in the absence of the veto the European Council members would act in their personal capacities, without any mandate when adopting the decision. This would undermine both the *telos* of Article 10 TEU and the constitutional identity of the Member States in the sense of Article 4(2) TEU. It would also be problematic to apply this interpretation to the special bridging clauses which do not include the parliamentary veto at EU level. Previous parliamentary consent would either be completely excluded here (no participation enabled by EU law) or left at the discretion of the national legislator (EU law prescribes no specific form of participation, therefore national law may step in), which would actually mean that the national law could establish a much stronger parliamentary control regarding the narrow special bridging clauses than the broad general bridging clauses. We therefore consider more convincing the approach that does not regard national procedures aiming at a stronger participation of the parliament in the activation of the general bridging as automatically contrary to EU law.

There is one caveat, however. The regulation of the previous consent or any other limitation of the actions of the national European Council representative should be rational in the sense that it would not establish super-rigid procedures aimed at creating hurdles that cannot be overcome.[11] Nonetheless, it is clear that it would be hard to precisely determine the boundary between rational and obstructive regulation and that the Member States could argue that such national procedures are part of their constitutional identity in the sense of Article 4(2) TEU.

[10]Niedobitek (2011), pp. 173–174. This position has also been advocated by the Dutch interior minister. S. Handelingen II of 17 June 2009, 96-7571 (see on this Besselink and Mourik (2012), p. 40).

[11]In this connection the United Kingdom's European Union Act 2011 with its numerous referendum requirements may be criticised as obstructive in its purpose. Cf. Craig (2011).

4.2 Initiative of the European Council

The initiative to activate the general bridging clause can be expected to have the form of a proposal for a decision of the European Council. It would most likely not be conceived and drafted at the European Council meeting itself, but discussed and negotiated beforehand (possibly also at the preparatory General Affairs Council etc.).

From a procedural point of view, the veto powers of the national Parliaments and the consent of the European Parliament mean that the content of the initiative of the European Council is not supposed to be changed before its adoption (apart from technical or purely language-related emendations). Any material change would constitute a new initiative requiring a new period of consideration in the national Parliaments and a new consent of the European Parliament. It could perhaps be argued that Article 48(7) of TEU and Article 6 of Protocol No. 1 speak of notifying or informing the national Parliaments merely of the "initiative", "before the decision is taken" and not of the draft decision itself. However, in practice, there is no room for vaguely formulated initiatives. The decision (and the initiative) has to determine which of the two general bridging clauses shall be activated (first or second subparagraph of Article 48(7) TEU or both) and to which provisions of the Treaties or individual cases the procedural change shall apply. This must be clearly stated in the initiative. Leaving any doubt as to the content of the final decision would likely complicate its adoption.

This also suggests that the very content of the initiative of the European Council must be unanimously agreed by its members, the Heads of State or Government of the Member States. If there were no agreement among the European Council members, it would be useless to initiate the procedure. This in turn provides room for making use of national accountability mechanisms between the representative in the European Council and the parliament. These can be utilized *before* the European Council initiates the procedure, i.e. the parliament may adopt a position on the initiative or even approve the representative's mandate. Discussing the possibility of activation of the bridging clause with the national Parliament this early may facilitate finding consensus on the content of the initiative as well as secure its smooth adoption.

The general procedures of parliamentary control of the national European Council representative vary substantially in the Member States. They are often based on general information duties of the executive towards the parliament in EU affairs and on parliamentary practice (typically a committee and/or plenary discussion before and/or after the European Council) rather than on specific rules.[12]

---

[12]See the detailed country reports in: European Parliament (2013), including its two annexes.

4.3 Veto Right of National Parliaments

4.3.1 Making Known the Opposition of the National Parliament to the European Council Initiative

The European Council notifies the national Parliaments of the initiative. The period in which a national Parliament may make known its opposition to the initiative is six months.[13] It is not regulated when precisely the period starts. For the sake of simplicity, it would be advisable to interpret this period as beginning on the date when the initiative has been notified to all national Parliaments in the official languages of the Union (i.e. the transmission of the last language version to all national Parliaments), which is the common rule in EU law.[14] The merit of this interpretation is also that the period would begin at the same date for all national Parliaments. If, within this six-month period, no Parliament makes known its opposition to the initiative (*nihil obstat*), the European Council is authorized to proceed with the initiative (fiction of consent of the national Parliaments—*Genehmigungsfiktion*). From the point of view of EU law, the national Parliaments need not give the consent or decide positively on the initiative (as opposed to the other revision procedures in Article 48 TEU).

The Treaty does not prescribe any formalities for the national parliamentary veto. As opposed to reasoned opinions regarding the principle of subsidiarity, there is no need to state the reasons of the veto[15] and there is no threshold of votes that must be reached in order to trigger the veto.[16] Each national Parliament can stop the

[13]See also Article 6 of Protocol No. 1.

[14]Both Article 4 of Protocol No. 1 (period between forwarding a draft legislative act to the national Parliaments and placing that draft legislative act on a provisional agenda for the Council for its adoption or for adoption of a position under a legislative procedure) and Article 6 of Protocol No. 2 (period for sending reasoned opinions regarding the principle subsidiarity by the national Parliaments) regulate the beginning of the period as the date when a draft legislative act has been made available to national Parliaments in the official languages of the Union.

[15]According to Article 3 of Protocol No. 1 and Article 6 of Protocol No. 2, the national Parliament has to state in its reasoned opinion why it considers that the draft legislative act does not comply with the principle of subsidiarity. Reasoned opinions without reasoning would not be counted as valid votes under the so-called early warning mechanism. Cf. Lupo, in Blanke and Mangiameli (2013), Protocol (No. 1), para. 53 (on Article 3 of the Protocol).

[16]The subsidiarity procedure requires reaching a threshold of one third (yellow card) or more than a half the votes of national parliaments or individual chambers in order to trigger further procedural steps by the Commission and other institutions. An unspecified threshold of negative parliamentary votes required for vetoing the use of general bridging clause was considered during the 2003 IGC. See: CIG 52/03 ADD 1 from 25 November 2003, p. 38; See also Grard, in Burgorgue-Larsen et al. (2007), Article IV-444, para. 8. This would have been highly impractical, because it would suggest that the European Council members acting unanimously may openly disregard the will of their own parliaments. Even one or a few parliamentary vetos would have probably led to a renegotiation of the decision in order to accommodate the position of the Member States concerned or to a failure to adopt the decision.

initiative under Article 48(7) TEU without having to justify why. Accordingly, the parliamentary veto right in the framework of the general bridging clauses can be labeled as the "red card".[17]

Moreover, only the national Parliaments themselves have the right to veto the initiative according to Article 48(7) TEU. The veto must be an actual expression of the will of the Parliament. If a national legal order requires holding a referendum in order to approve a Treaty revision, it does not affect the procedure for activation of the general bridging clause in the TEU. A negative outcome of a referendum on the activation of the bridging clause would have to be translated into a veto of the national Parliament or into a negative vote of the representative in the European Council (as a binding mandate).[18] In other words, the national law would have to determine the effects of the referendum on the duties of the constitutional bodies acting within the framework of Article 48(7) TEU.

Furthermore, the right of a national Parliament to express the opposition to an initiative under Article 48(7) TEU is granted to them by EU law.[19] This means that a national Parliament may invoke it directly vis-à-vis other state organs.[20] On the basis of the primacy of EU law, this right cannot be abolished or curtailed by national law, including national constitutional law.[21] A hypothetical national law that would make the casting of the veto conditional upon consent of the government or upon other circumstances beyond the power of the parliament would have to be regarded as contrary to EU law (not mentioning its possible conflict with national constitutional law). On the other hand, detailed procedural rules for deciding on the

[17]Not to be confused with the proposed general "red card" for national Parliaments in the EU legislative procedure that was rejected at the Convention and subsequently revived in 2016 in the draft agreement aimed at settling the requests of the United Kingdom had it not voted for leaving the EU. See Blanke and Böttner (2015), p. 261 f.

[18]Similarly Peers (2012), p. 78.

[19]Cremer, in Calliess and Ruffert (2016), Artikel 48 EUV, para. 14.

[20]Ohler, in Grabitz et al. (2011), Artikel 48 EUV, para. 49; Franzius, in Pechstein et al. (2017), Artikel 48 EUV, para. 58. The French *Conseil Constitutionnel*, in its decision on the constitutionality of the Treaty establishing a Constitution for Europe, was of a different opinion and required a revision of the French Constitution in order to allow the parliament to exercise the veto under Article 48(7) TEU. See Case no. 2004-505 DC, decision of 19 October 2004, ECLI:FR:CC:2004:2004.505.DC, para. 41: "Considérant que le droit reconnu au Parlement français de s'opposer à une modification du traité selon le mode simplifié prévu par l'article IV-444 rend nécessaire une révision de la Constitution afin de permettre l'exercice de cette prerogative." Similarly Barrett (2013), pp. 182–183 refers to the veto right as a "facilitative invitation" to "permit national parliaments to decide on whether or not to exercise veto power over Article 48(7) Treaty amendments", which "must be accepted by each national system" and thus "national parliaments must be enabled to exercise this discretion by the relevant national rules applying to them and by the political parties which control their operation". In our opinion, the veto may be exercised even if it is not addressed in the national law at all. The possibility to exercise the veto does not depend on any permission by national law, same as the participation of members of a Member State's government in the Council.

[21]European Court of Justice, Case 11/70, *Internationale Handelsgesellschaft*, decision of 17 December 1970, ECLI:EU:C:1970:114, para. 3 f.

veto in the parliament, which prescribe quora for attendance and votes required to cast the veto etc. are no doubt compatible with EU law (with the possible reservation made in the concluding paragraph of Sect. 4.1 above). It is left to national law to establish the procedure for exercising the veto. In most Member States with a unicameral parliament, this would follow the general procedure for debating draft EU acts, where usually a committee (in this case possibly the EU affairs committee) formulates the position and presents it to the plenary session for approval.[22] In the absence of special rules, the veto would have the form of a resolution of the parliament adopted by a simple majority provided that the minimum number of Members of Parliament is in attendance.

4.3.2 National Procedures in Bicameral Parliamentary Systems

A special situation is the case of bicameral parliaments. Thirteen out of the (currently) 28 Member States of the Union have a bicameral system, i.e. a parliamentary system with two chambers.[23] Historically, the term "second chamber" described the lower house of a two-chamber system.[24] The lower house is that chamber of parliament that represents the citizens on the basis of equality and whose representatives are chosen on the basis of a direct general election.[25] Nowadays, the role of the chamber of the people has increased significantly in the national constitutional systems. Therefore it is usually the upper house that is now referred to as the "second chamber" and this is the meaning which is used in this section. The second chamber is thus a body that is formally and functionally considered part of the national "parliament" and which is involved in legislation but which is not necessarily directly (or at all) elected and does not have to represent all citizens equally.[26] The existence of a second parliamentary chamber is usually justified

[22]The national rules addressing the procedural issues of casting the veto in Member States with unicameral parliaments are mostly limited to a reference to the competence of the plenary session to cast the veto. See e.g. **Croatia**: Article 12 of the Act on the Co-Operation of the Croatian Parliament and the Government of the Republic of Croatia in European Affairs; **Estonia**: Article 152 of the Riigikogu Rules of Procedure and Internal Rules Act, **Finland**: Section 30 and 32 of the Parliament's Rules of Procedure; **Hungary**: Section 72 of Act XXXVI/2012 on the National Assembly and Section 144 of Resolution 10/2014 on Certain Provisions of the Rules of Procedure; **Lithuania**: § 180[5] of the Statute of the Seimas; **Sweden**: Chapter 9, Article 20 of the Riksdag Act.

[23]These are Austria, Belgium, Czech Republic, France, Germany, Ireland, Italy, the Netherlands, Poland, Romania, Slovenia, Spain and the United Kingdom. Both Denmark and Sweden have abandoned bicameralism several years before their accession to the European Communities and the Union respectively.

[24]See the names of the chambers of the States-General in the Netherlands.

[25]For an overview, see Groß (2003), p. 31 f.

[26]Cf. Schwarz-Liebermann von Wahlendorf (1958), p. V; Haas (2010), p. 3; Hölscheidt, in Grabitz et al. (2013), Artikel 12 EUV, para. 25.

historically and as a counterweight and a corrective momentum to the people's chamber, that sometimes may be too carried away by public opinion.[27] For that reason, it is sometimes referred to as *chambre de réflexion*. In addition or as an alternative they may be designed as a representation of important social structures in the state, such as territorial units (states in a federation, autonomous units, regions, municipalities), professions or national minorities that would not be adequately reflected under the general and equal voting right to the first chamber.

In the context of parliamentary involvement in the procedure for the adoption of the bridging clauses, there is one important open issue that has to be addressed in bicameral parliaments. According to Article 6 and 8 of the Protocol No. 1, the European Council has to notify of its initiative each parliamentary chamber of a bicameral parliament individually. However, the Treaties remain silent on the issue whether the veto can be exercised by any chamber individually, or whether it has to be exercised by the bicameral parliament as a whole.

The first approach (treating each chamber as a separate entity) applies in EU law to all the information duties under Articles 1 to 7 of Protocol No. 1 (according to Article 8 of Protocol No. 1) as well as to the subsidiarity control procedure, where each parliamentary chamber of a bicameral parliament disposes of one vote and each parliament as a whole of two votes.[28] It may be argued that this is the general attitude of EU law towards bicameral parliaments.[29] There is however no explicit rule to that effect regarding the veto right under Article 48(7) TEU. To fill this gap by means of interpretation would mean to extend the applicability of a rule regarding information rights, which have a relatively low impact on the national constitutional systems, to the much more politically and constitutionally salient decision-making rights of national Parliaments. This is notwithstanding the fact that many EU Member States with bicameral parliaments involve both chambers (in various ways and to different extent) in the ratification procedures regarding international treaties. As far as the parallel with the subsidiarity control is concerned, it is true that this "early warning" procedure cannot be reduced to a mere information duty towards national Parliaments. Still, it is a structured dialogue on matters of subsidiarity between the national Parliaments and EU institutions and not a procedure for EU decision-making *by* national Parliaments. Furthermore, the subsidiarity check is focused on the exercise of EU competence in the light of the principle of subsidiarity, which is especially relevant for second chambers representing the subnational territorial or societal level[30] which can be particularly affected by violations of the principle of subsidiarity. Article 48(7) TEU, on the other hand, is preoccupied with "frame of government" issues in the form of simplification of decision-making procedures, which can lead to a passage from unanimity to qualified majority and open the possibility of a Member State being

[27]Cf. Schüttemeyer and Sturm (1992); Groß (2003), p. 46 f.

[28]Article 3 of Protocol No. 1 and Article 7(1)(2) of Protocol No. 2.

[29]See also Gamper (2011), pp. 245–247 and 254–256.

[30]See Haas (2010), p. 3 ff.

outvoted in further areas of EU competence. Because there is no threshold number of national Parliaments' votes required to veto the initiative under Article 48(7) TEU, any national Parliament may frustrate the adoption of the decision. If we interpreted the veto power as a right of each parliamentary chamber, we would increase the number of veto-players even more and make the procedure extremely rigid, akin to full revision of the Treaties. It would also mean that there would be more "veto players" in bicameral systems than in unicameral ones.

This adds to the strength of the second approach, i.e. that the veto right can only be exercised by the national Parliament as a whole, as expressed in the wording of Article 48(7) TEU. We conclude that for the purpose of Article 48(7) TEU, the national Parliament is to be regarded as a single institution that only has one "vote" to make known its opposition to the initiative.[31] It is up to the national law to determine the how both chambers participate and cooperate to this end.[32] Thus, European and national law complement each other in a system of "multilevel constitutionalism".[33]

The national law can either require an agreement of the chambers on the veto, or entrust the exercise of the veto permanently to one of the two chambers (most likely the first chamber). The second arrangement may mirror the division of powers between the chambers in the process of ratification of international agreements, which arguably forms part of the fundamental constitutional structure of the Member State that must be respected by the Union according to Article 4(2) TEU. This begs the question: Can we take one step further? Could national law provide that if *any* one of the two chambers passes a negative resolution on the bridging clause initiative, the parliament as a whole is obliged to formally cast the veto? Formally, this would not be contrary to EU law, because the European Council would receive one negative vote from the parliament as a whole. On the other hand, it would in effect circumvent the "one parliament—one veto" rule which results from our interpretation. For now, this remains a hypothetical problem, because no Member State has adopted an express rule to this effect in its national law.

Meanwhile, the legal situation in the Member States with bicameral parliaments is varied.

---

[31]The same conclusion is reached by UK House of Lords, Select Committee on European Union, Tenth Report (February 2008), Point 3.16; Casalena, in Blanke and Mangiameli (2013), Protocol (No. 1), para. 95 (on Article 6 of the Protocol); Öhlinger and Potacs (2014), p. 27, Gamper (2011), p. 245. A different opinion is expressed by Peers (2012), p. 78, who deduces from the absence of an express rule for bicameral parliaments that it is up to the Member States to decide how and by which chamber the veto right should be exercised.

[32]This has been overlooked by Olivetti, in Blanke and Mangiameli (2013), Article 12 TEU, para. 74, who holds that an interpretation, according to which only both chambers together can cast the veto, "could have the paradoxical consequence that the opposition of a popularly elected lower Chamber, without the consent on it of a non-elected upper Chamber [...] would not satisfy the requirement established by Art. 48.7 TEU and Art. 81.3 TFEU to block the use of the 'passerelle clause'."

[33]Olivetti, in Blanke and Mangiameli (2013), Article 12 TEU, para. 97.

4.3.2.1 Predominance of a Parliamentary Chamber

In the Parliament of **Slovenia**, only the first chamber, the *Državni zbor* (National Assembly) decides on the exercise of the veto right under Article 48(7) TEU, on the basis of a committee report. The second chamber, *Državni svet* (National Council) has to be informed of such motion and has the right to adopt its own position in the matter, which is, however, not binding upon the National Assembly.[34] This is in accord with the role of the National Council in the Slovenian constitutional system in general (a body providing advice, initiative or control to the National Assembly) and with its role in EU affairs in particular.[35]

A formally asymmetrical participation of both chambers can also be found in **Austria**. Article 23i(2) of the Federal Constitutional Law prescribes that the National Council with the consent of the Federal Council can oppose the initiative according to Article 48(7) TEU. The National Council adopts the decision by a simple majority under attendance of at least one third of its members.[36] Both chambers have to cooperate and reach an agreement, but the veto can only be initiated by the first chamber.[37]

4.3.2.2 Exercise of the Veto by the Parliament as a Whole

The **French** *Congrès* makes known its opposition to the initiative, if both chambers adopt a negative position (Art. 88-7 of the Constitution). For this purpose, either *Assemblée nationale* or *Sénat* puts the initative to vote and in case the initiative is rejected, informs the other chamber.[38] If the other chamber concurs with the negative position, a declaration to that effect is delivered to the European Council.

---

[34] Article 154o of the Rules of Procedure of the National Assembly; see also Article 97 of the Constitution. The Slovenian Constitutional Court (Decision of 18.10.2012, U-I-17/11, ECLI:SI: USRS:2012:U.I.17.11) is of the opinion that EU law does not regulate how the two chambers in bicameral system should participate and cooperate and, accordingly, that this question can be answered by the national legislator.

[35] See e.g. Vehar (2007), p. 242 f.; Mavčič (2014), p. 1492. The very limited participation of the National Council in EU affairs extends even to the subsidiarity check, where the National Assembly assumes the right to cast both votes of the Slovenian Parliament. This has not been disputed by the European Commission despite the obvious conflict with the aforementioned rules of Article 7 of Protocol No. 2, probably due to the regard for the specific constitutional system of Slovenia. However, the prevalent opinion seems to rule out the possibility to entrust both votes in the subsidiarity check procedure to one chamber of a bicameral parliament. See. e.g. Gamper (2011), p. 247 and Kiiver (2012), pp. 64–66.

[36] See also Öhlinger and Potacs (2014), pp. 25–27.

[37] As opposed to Article 41(1) of the Constitution, according to which the Federal Council can propose domestic legislation.

[38] See Article 151-12 of the Rules of Procedure of the National Assembly and Article 73 *decies* of the Standing Orders of the Senate.

In **Italy**, the procedure is regulated by the Law No. 234/2012 of 24 December 2012 on general rules on Italy's participation in formation and implementation of EU legislation and policies. According to its Article 11(5), both chambers, *Camera dei Deputati* and *Senato*, put the initiative to vote independently of each other. In order to exercise the veto, both chambers have to adopt a negative position on the initiative. The resolutions do not have to have identical texts, it is only necessary that there is no doubt that the chambers' positions on the initiative are negative.[39]

The **Romanian** legal order includes no special rules on the parliamentary participation in the general bridging clauses. However, Act No. 373/2013 on cooperation between the Parliament and the Government in the field of European affairs addresses in general the problem of conflicting resolutions of the *Camera Deputaţilor* and the *Senat* in EU affairs. According to Article 3(3), in such case the Government "shall ask the Parliament for a joint resolution on the provisions bearing a conflicting content, within a time-limit established in consultation with the two Chambers". If no joint resolution is adopted, the Government, according to Article 3(4), "shall be not under a duty to take into account the conflicting provisions in drawing up the general mandate." These rules apply to the effects of the chambers' positions towards the Government, but they could possibly also be applied to the bridging clause veto, in absence of specific provisions. However, the situation is not entirely clear and the available scholarly studies do not address this problem.

In **Spain**, both chambers of the *Cortes Generales* participate in a joint EU affairs committee. If proposed by the *Congreso de los Diputados* or the *Senado*, the joint committee debates initiatives based on Article 48(7) TEU and prepares a report, which is then put to a vote separately in both chambers. Only if both chambers adopt a negative position on the initiative the veto shall be communicated to the European Council.[40]

As already mentioned, the **United Kingdom** considers the reference to "national parliament" in Article 48(7) TEU to be a reference to the institution as a whole.[41] Accordingly, the application of the bridging clause can only be vetoed if both the *House of Lords* and the *House of Commons* agree on the negative position. The veto procedure is not further elaborated in UK law as there are other safeguards in place (see Sect. 4.5).

What are the consequences of the aforementioned rules? The design of the national regulation of cooperation between the two parliamentary chambers for the purpose of casting the veto has to be measured against the powers of the chambers in the ratification of international treaties. In all bicameral systems of the EU,

---

[39]See Rossi, in Costato et al. (2015), Articolo 11, pp. 122–125; Esposito (2013).

[40]Article 3(l) in connection with Article 8 of the Law 8/1994 regulating the Joint Parliamentary European Union Committee (as amended by Law 24/2009) in connection with Article 10 of the Resolution of the Bureaus of the Congress of Deputies and the Senate of 21 September 1995 developing Law 8/1994 (as amended by Resolution of 27 May 2010).

[41]Cf. UK House of Lords, Select Committee on European Union, Tenth Report (February 2008), Point 3.16.

ratification of important international treaties requires the consent of either both chambers or at least of the lower chamber of parliament (in the form of a law or in another form). This means that one or both chambers have a separate "veto" power against the government, which gives the respective chamber a much stronger position than in the national procedures implementing the veto right under Article 48(7) TEU. In case of the general bridging clause, if at least one chamber agrees with the proposal to utilize the bridging clause, no veto is cast. This strengthens the position of the national European Council representative in the first place. The weaker role of the parliament can be rationalized as commensurate to the limited scope of the treaty amendment possible under Article 48(7) TEU. On the other hand, even if no agreement on the exercise of the veto is reached, the government may be dissuaded from the adoption of the European Council decision by a negative position of one of the chambers, especially if it is the chamber to which the government is accountable (usually only the first chamber).

4.3.2.3 Exercise of the Veto by Each Chamber Individually

There are Member States that expressly allow both chambers independently to cast the veto, which, according to our interpretation is contrary to Article 48(7) TEU.

In **German** law, there are two alternatives. Which of them applies depends on the content of the initiative to active the bridging clause. If the initiative concerns mainly those areas of EU policy that, on the national level, would belong in the exclusive legislative competence of the Federation, the veto right is exercised by a vote in the *Bundestag*. In all other cases, both the *Bundestag* and the *Bundesrat* may individually veto the initiative.[42] The law makes no provision on the possible coordination between both bodies.

The situation in **Poland** is similar to the second variant in Germany. The veto may be cast by each chamber independently. In both *Sejm* and *Senat*, the committee responsible for EU affairs may present such proposal to the plenary, which decides on the exercise of the veto. No coordination between the chambers is necessary or prescribed.[43]

In the **Czech Republic**, the exercise of the veto right is regulated together with the previous consent procedure (see Sect. 4.5). The Government must obtain the consent of both chambers—*Poslanecká sněmovna* and *Senát*—in order to be able to vote for the adoption of the decision of the European Council—similarly to the situation in the United Kingdom. When this procedure was being adopted,[44] an interpretation has been put forward in the explanatory memorandum of the bill that

---

[42]Section 10(1) of the Act on the Exercise by the Bundestag and by the Bundesrat of their Responsibility for Integration in Matters concerning the European Union.

[43]Article 148ca of the Standing Orders of the Sejm and Article 75f and 75g of the Rules and Regulations of the Senate.

[44]The so-called Lisbon Amendment to the rules of procedure of both chambers, Act No. 162/2009 Coll.

despite the establishment of a stricter previous consent procedure the chambers could also make use of the veto power directly based on Article 48(7) TEU and that the veto can be cast by each chamber independently.[45] In both chambers' rules of procedure, it is possible, in the framework of the procedure for granting the previous consent to the Government (where the Government asks for the consent), that a member of the chamber or the committee responsible also proposes the rejection or expression of disapproval with the initiative. If and only if this motion to reject is adopted within the six-month period by the plenary in any one chamber, it shall be communicated as the parliamentary veto under Article 48(7) TEU (i.e. merely not granting the previous consent does not amount to a veto according to these rules).[46] Consequently, there is no procedure for conciliation between the chambers in case of differing positions (only a duty to inform the other chamber of the resolution). It has to be added that there is not even a general requirement for the chambers to cooperate in EU affairs, although the Czech Constitution[47] offers the possibility to delegate the chambers' powers related to EU affairs to a joint body of both chambers. Since the Czech Republic's accession to the European Union, the establishment of this body has not been considered, mainly because it would entail many practical problems (relative powers of both chambers, modes of decision-making, schedule collisions) and limit the autonomy of the chambers that has meanwhile developed in this area. It has never been discussed in particular relation to Article 48(7) TEU or the other simplified revision procedures.

The **Irish** *Oireachtas*, despite being a bicameral parliament, establishes many joint committees. These are a special feature of Irish parliamentarism.[48] However in case of Article 48(7) TEU, both the *Dáil* and the *Seanad* vote separately on the exercise of the veto,[49] on the basis of the reports and motions of their respective committees.[50]

---

[45] *Důvodová zpráva* (explanatory memorandum) to the draft bill that ended up being adopted as the above mentioned act, Chamber of Deputies Print No. 742 from the 5th Term (2006–2010). The explanatory memorandum is ambiguous because it mixes the exercise of the veto and the previous consent, presenting the previous consent as a procedure to express the veto, and in one place even mentions that the veto would require a positive decision of both chambers, thus contradicting itself. This is probably due to the fact that the bill was drafted in cooperation of both chambers that did not always have the same views (although a good part of the provisions is materially identical in both rules of procedure). The Senate's Permanent Commission for the Constitution of the Czech Republic and Parliamentary Procedure considered the question whether the veto right may be exercised in a bicameral system by each chamber or only by the whole parliament to be insufficiently addressed in EU law (Resolution No. 7 of 27 March 2008).

[46] Sections 109j and 109k (especially paragraph 4) in connection with Section 109i(c) of the Rules of Procedure of the Chamber of Deputies, Sections 119m and 119n (especially paragraph 4) of the Standing Rules of the Senate.

[47] Article 10b(3) of the Constitution.

[48] Barrett (2015), p. 295.

[49] Article 7(1) of the European Union Act 2009.

[50] See also Article 115 of the Standing Orders of the *Dáil*; Article 117 of the Standing Orders of the *Seanad*. See also Barrett (2013), p. 200 et seq.

In the **Netherlands**, legal regulation of participation of the *Staten–Generaal* in EU affairs is very limited.[51] Both chambers are apparently cautious to preserve their independence of each other and therefore there is no formal conciliatory or consensus-building procedure between the *Tweede Kamer* and the *Eerste Kamer*.[52] The general approach towards ratification of international obligations in the Netherlands is to require the adoption of a law (which has to be approved by both chambers). Therefore it seems that each chamber could exercise the veto in Article 48(7) TEU individually. In practice, however, the chambers of *Staten–Generaal* strive for a coordinated approach in EU affairs, e.g. by adopting identical resolutions containing reasoned opinions in the framework of the subsidiarity control mechanism from time to time.

If, in the aforementioned Member States, both chambers of a parliament deliver separately a negative vote within the six-month period, the initiative would be vetoed (by the parliament as a whole) when the second of the two chambers made known its opposition. It may be advisable for the one chamber to wait for the decision of the other chamber and communicate both negative resolutions at the same time. However, there is, in our opinion, no reason from the point of view of EU law to insist that both chambers act jointly in order to cast a valid veto, if both chambers clearly expressed their opposition.

The question is what happens if, in any of the aforementioned Member States, only one parliamentary chamber made known its opposition to the initiative according to Article 48(7) TEU, not communicating on behalf of the whole parliament. In our opinion (as explained above), this would not amount to a valid veto and, should all other conditions be fulfilled, the European Council could proceed with the adoption of the decision. On behalf of whom the chamber actually acts may require some interpretation of the document delivered by the chamber. The chamber casting the veto could e.g. state in a cover letter that according to the national law their resolution constitutes the opposition of the parliament as a whole. However, without there being an express rule to that effect in the national law, as is the case in all the Member States that allow both chambers to cast the veto individually,[53] this would not be convincing from the point of view of the interpretation we favour. To complicate the matters even more, the other chamber of the parliament could react to the negative decision of the one chamber by not debating the initiative any further under the logic that even if it adopted a positive resolution, it would, under national law, produce no legal effect (as in cases where the consent of both chambers is required to adopt a certain decision and one chamber votes not to give its consent). Such tacit reaction could of course not count as an opposition of the other chamber, because that would be contrary to the logic of the *nihil obstat*

[51]Cf. Högenauer (2015), pp. 253–254.

[52]Besselink and Mourik (2012), p. 31.

[53]As opposed to the aforementioned rules in Austria, Slovenia and Germany (in cases where only the *Bundestag* decides on the veto), where the national law makes it clear which chamber acts on behalf of the parliament as a whole.

procedure. All the problems outlined here document the necessity of national rules on cooperation of the chambers or at least of the awareness of the members of parliament on the effects of their actions from the perspective of EU law.

Fortunately, the problematic situation of only one chamber casting the veto and the European Council adopting the decision regardless is probably not very likely to happen because at least in Germany, the Czech Republic, Ireland and Poland, the representative in the European Council may not agree with the adoption of the decision unless the national Parliament gave its consent first (see Sect. 4.5 below). Even in the other bicameral Member States, the representative could find itself politically forced to oppose the adoption of the decision in the European Council.

In any event, a decision under Article 48(7) TEU adopted in this special situation could be challenged before the European Court of Justice under Article 263 TFEU for reason of infringement of an essential procedural requirements. The European Council decision under Article 48(7) TEU is an act "intended to produce legal effects *vis-à-vis* third parties", as Article 263(1) TFEU requires. Possible claimants could be the European Commission, which does not play a role in the procedure under 48(7) TEU, or the European Parliament as European parliamentary institution with *locus standi*. Nonetheless, based on our interpretation, the Court of Justice would have to come to the conclusion that no effective national veto had been cast as no national Parliament as a whole opposed the initiative.

4.3.2.4 The Case of Belgium

One last issue related to the Article 48(7) TEU veto right is the special constitutional arrangement of **Belgium**, that is reflected in the Declaration No. 51 attached to the Treaties. In accordance with Belgium's constitutional law, not only the Chamber of Representatives and Senate of the Federal Parliament but also the parliamentary assemblies of the Communities (Parliament of the French Community, Parliament of the German-speaking Community) and the Regions (Flemish Parliament, Parliament of Wallonia, Brussels Parliament) act, in terms of the competences exercised by the Union, as components of the national parliamentary system or chambers of the national Parliament. This is a more complicated situation than in the other bicameral systems. While it may be argued that if EU law expressly acknowledges the particularities of the Belgian parliamentary system, this may justify a special approach to the exercise of Belgian parliamentary veto under Article 48(7) TEU, there is no special rule to that effect in EU law.

In Belgian national law, for the purpose of subsidiarity control, an agreement on cooperation among all seven parliaments has been concluded.[54] According to the principle *in foro interno, in foro externo*, the sub-national entities exercise

[54]Accord de coopération entre les Chambres législatives fédérales, les parlements des Communautés et les parlements des Régions visant la mise en oeuvre du Protocole sur l'application des principes de subsidiarité et de proportionnalité, 19 December 2005.

competence in foreign affairs related to areas where they have competence in internal matters. The two votes of the Belgian parliament are distributed among the seven parliaments according to a predetermined key depending on whether the issue affects the competence of the Federation, the Communities or the Regions.[55] A coordination agreement for the purpose of Article 48(7) TEU has not yet been reached, but is being debated. It could be of similar nature as the agreement on subsidiarity control. The difference is that while the subsidiarity agreement enables the sub-national parliaments to voice their concerns directly to the Commission, an agreement on the exercise of the veto power could have an inverse effect (i.e. parliamentary chambers at one level of government could block the use of veto sought by parliamentary chambers of the other level, thus perhaps undermining the purpose of Declaration No. 51). Alternatively, the veto right could be assigned to any chamber concerned with the other chambers being obliged to comply and declare jointly the opposition of the Belgium's "parliamentary structure" to the bridging clause initiative. However, this runs into the problem of "many parliamentary veto players" discussed above. The 2016 circumstances surrounding the signature of the EU-Canada Comprehensive Economic and Trade Agreement (CETA), i.e. the opposition of the Walloon Parliament threatening the failure of negotiations, illustrated this problem vividly. It is therefore not unlikely that a different pattern of exercise of the veto will be sought. In cases where only the federal competence is concerned, it is noteworthy that the chambers of the Federal Parliament establish a joint advisory committee on EU affairs (*Comité d'avis fédéral chargé des questions européennes*),[56] which could serve as the decision-making or coordinating forum for the exercise of the veto right.

4.4 Participation of the European Parliament

As another step in the procedure, the initiative under Article 48(7) TEU has to be submitted to the European Parliament. Provided that no national Parliament vetoes the initiative, the European Council may adopt the decision activating the bridging clauses only after the European Parliament has given its consent. For this purpose, the European Parliament does not decide by its default voting procedure of simple majority (majority of votes cast) as provided by Article 231 TFEU, but instead by the majority of its component members (absolute majority). This more rigid requirement for consent underlines the importance of the decision as well as the greater need for (European) democratic legitimation.

The Treaty is silent on any details regarding the submission of the initiative to the European Parliament. According to Article 15(6)(d) of the TEU, the President of the European Council is under the obligation to present a report to the European

[55]Instructively explained in Popelier and Lemmens (2015), p. 71 ff.; Deschouwer (2012), p. 54 ff.; Swenden et al. (2006), p. 865 ff.

[56]See Delreux and Randour (2015), p. 155 ff.

Parliament after each of the meetings of the European Council, but this cannot be considered a formal submission of an initiative for consent. For the sake of clarity, the European Council should make known to the European Parliament the initiative under Article 48(7) TEU at the same time it informs the national Parliaments. This puts the European Parliament in the position to deliberate on the initiative simultaneously with the national Parliaments.

The Treaty does not determine any timeframe within which the European Parliament must act. As the European Council must wait on the lapse of the six-month period for national Parliaments, the European Parliament has at least the same time frame for consideration. This enables the European Parliament to discuss the matter with the national Parliaments within an interparliamentary forum such as COSAC which shall promote the exchange of information and best practice without prejudging the respective positions of the European or national Parliaments (Article 10 of Protocol No. 1).[57] On the other hand, by granting consent early in the six-month period, the European Parliament could exert pressure on the national Parliaments contemplating the use of the veto and perhaps discourage them from doing so.

Effective parliamentary participation is indispensible for the institutional balance intended by the Treaties. As the European Court of Justice puts it, "it reflects [...] the fundamental democratic principle that the peoples should take part in the exercise of power through the intermediary of a representative assembly".[58] Conversely, the European Parliament is under the obligation to cooperate sincerely with the other institutions (Article 13(2) TEU). In cases of mere parliamentary consultation, the failure to comply with this duty authorises the other institutions to proceed without parliamentary participation.[59] However, due to the democratic implications of the requirement for parliamentary *consent*, this case-law may not be applied to this situation. The consent of the European Parliament is an essential procedural requirement, the disregard of which justifies an action for annulment and leads to the nullity of the decision.

However, the requirement for the European Parliament to give its consent does not mean that it can block an initiative ad infinitum by merely not taking a decision at all (pocket veto). The aforementioned duty to cooperate sincerely obliges Parliament to decide on the matter by giving its consent or rejecting an initiative. As ultimate sanction, the European Council could formally call upon the European Parliament to act and, following another two months of continued omission to do

[57] Granat (2016), p. 84 ff.

[58] On the consultation procedure, see the so called "Isoglucose" cases, European Court of Justice, Case 138/79, *Roquette Frères v. Council,* judgment of 29 October 1980, ECLI:EU:C:1980:249, para. 33; Case 139/79, *Maizena v. Council*, judgment of 29 October 1980, ECLI:EU:C:1980:250, para. 34; see also Case C-65/93, *Parliament v. Council*, judgment of 30 March 1995. ECLI:EU:C:1995:91, para. 21.

[59] Cf. European Court of Justice, Case C-65/93, *Parliament v. Council*, judgment of 30 March 1995. ECLI:EU:C:1995:91, para. 26 f.

so, the European Council could bring an action before the European Court of Justice against the European Parliament for failure to act (Article 265 TFEU).

In any event, the consent of the European Parliament is constitutive for any decision under Article 48(7) TEU. Therefore, the European Parliament can use this as a political lever. If the European Council were to decide to simply change the voting requirements in the Council (unanimity to qualified majority) without upgrading the status of Parliament within a special legislative procedure, it can deny its consent unless the other passerelle is used which changes to the ordinary legislative procedure with equal participation of the European Parliament.

4.5 Adopting the Decision in the European Council

4.5.1 General Remarks

Under the condition that no national Parliament has vetoed the initiative and that the European Parliament has given its consent, the European Council can vote on the decision activating the bridging clause. For that purpose, the European Council decides by unanimity and not by its default procedure, i.e. consensus (Article 15(4) TEU). While decision making by consensus does not require a formal vote, unanimity generally means that all members of the decision-making body vote in the affirmative.[60] In the case of the European Council, it is not required that all members cast a positive vote. It only means that there are no negative votes, since Article 235(1)(3) TFEU provides that abstentions by members present in person or represented shall not prevent the adoption by the European Council of acts which require unanimity. Due to the requirement of a unanimous European Council decision and the possibility of a parliamentary veto (both by the European Parliament an every single national Parliament), the procedure under Article 48(7) TEU amounts to a sort of "double unanimity".[61]

Apart from this, it should be noted that the decision to activate a bridging clause is intergovernmental, as it is made by the (currently 28) Heads of State or Government only. Despite the fact that the President of the European Commission and the President of the European Council are also members of the European Council (sentence 1 of Article 15(2) TEU), they shall not take part in the vote where the European Council decides by vote (and not by consensus) (sentence 2 of Article 235(1)(2) TFEU). The role under Article 48(7) TEU of the European Commission as the genuine supranational institution is therefore—through its president—only of a consultative nature.

---

[60] Cf. Edjaharian, in Blanke and Mangiameli (2013), Article 15 TEU, para. 62.

[61] Böttner (2016), p. 509.

4.5.2 Possible Further Participation of National Parliaments

From the point of view of European law, Member States are not barred from establishing requirements in their domestic law for the activation of the bridging clauses that exceed the requirements laid down in Article 48(7) TEU (excessive domestic law). From the point of view of domestic law, the lack of the ratification of the Treaty amendments by national Parliaments may result in the requirement to find other safeguards in order to ensure democratic legitimation as required by national law.[62]

Some arguments may speak against additional domestic regulation. The argument that the parliamentary veto according to Article 48(7) TEU precludes other forms of parliamentary control over the representative in the European Council has already been discussed above (Sect. 4.1).

Moreover, a doubling of procedures of parliamentary consent may appear illogical, if one assumes that a national Parliament which denies the mandate for its national representative in the European Council could as well just have prevented the decision in the European Council directly via a parliamentary veto that is explicitly foreseen in Article 48(7) TEU. However, a two-tier procedure can be advisable for a number of reasons mostly related to facilitating a clear, democratically legitimate decision.

We could argue that where there is no parliamentary majority to veto an initiative under Article 48(7) TEU, conversely, there must be—theoretically—a parliamentary majority for the application of the bridging clause or the granting of a mandate for the European Council member, respectively. But the absence of the veto can have a different cause. First, it is possible that the national Parliament is for whatever reason not able to find and articulate a position. The possibility that the Parliament would not be in session or would suffer from continuous obstruction for six months can probably be ruled out as merely hypothetical. On the other hand, the Parliament (or one of its chambers) could be unexpectedly dissolved before the end of the six-month period, which would prevent it from debating and casting the veto. In the absence of a procedure for casting the veto in national law, the majority in the Parliament could even deny putting the motion for a veto on the agenda within the six-month time limit in order to divest itself of the responsibility for the decision or to prevent a politically explosive debate harming the government. Regardless of the fact that such cases are unlikely to occur, the previous consent procedure ensures a parliamentary debate prior to the adoption of the European Council decision and a clear expression of the will of the parliament, thus adding to the clarity and democratic legitimacy of the national position.[63]

---

[62]Cf. Wendel (2011), p. 225.

[63]There is, however, the risk that it leads to an opposite obstruction, because the necessity to obtain the consent of the parliament extends beyond the six-month period in Article 48(7) TEU. In order to avoid this, the motion to grant the consent should be put to vote within this time limit.

In this context one should view the case law of the German Federal Constitutional Court. According to the Court, the procedure under Article 48(7) TEU leads to changes in primary law with the effect that the national representative in the Council loses influence with the loss of his veto position when decision making shifts from the principle of unanimity to the principle of qualified majority in the decision making of the Council. This transition is to be assessed pursuant to Article 23(1) second sentence of the Basic Law.[64] The right of national Parliaments to oppose an initiative under Article 48(7) TEU is regarded by the Court as no sufficient equivalent to the requirement of ratification in the Member States. The Court concludes therefore that under German constitutional law, approval by the representative of the German government in the European Council (or in the Council for special bridging clauses) always requires a law within the meaning of Article 23(1) second sentence, and if necessary third sentence, of the Basic Law. It is only in this way that the German legislative bodies exercise their responsibility for integration in a given case and also decide whether the level of democratic legitimation is still high enough to accept the majority decision.[65]

The Czech Constitutional Court, while not raising doubts about the constitutionality of the Lisbon Treaty, suggested that because the procedures under Article 48(6) and (7) TEU presume the intervention of national Parliaments, the Government, as the sponsor of the Lisbon Treaty, should propose relevant procedures on the domestic level in order to clearly define the role that the individual chambers of Parliament will play, and their relationship to each other.[66] With the same or similar considerations, a number of national legal orders have adopted particular procedures of previous parliamentary consent for the application of the bridging clauses (see Sect. 4.5.3 below).

This does not mean that in the other Member States, where neither a previous consent of the Parliament nor a parliamentary adoption of a legally binding mandate is required for the representative in the European Council to be able to agree on the adoption of the decision pursuant to Article 48(7) TEU, the representative is free to act independently of the Parliament. As already mentioned above (Chap 1 and Sect. 4.1), in all EU Member States the Parliaments are at least entitled to debate proposed EU acts and policies and (by virtue of their autonomy) express their

[64]Article 23(1) of the Basic Law reads: "With a view to establishing a united Europe, the Federal Republic of Germany shall participate in the development of the European Union that is committed to democratic, social and federal principles, to the rule of law, and to the principle of subsidiarity, and that guarantees a level of protection of basic rights essentially comparable to that afforded by this Basic Law. To this end the Federation may transfer sovereign powers by a law with the consent of the Bundesrat. The establishment of the European Union, as well as changes in its treaty foundations and comparable regulations that amend or supplement this Basic Law, or make such amendments or supplements possible, shall be subject to paragraphs (2) and (3) of Article 79".

[65]German Federal Constitutional Court, 2 BvE 2/08 and others, *Treaty of Lisbon*, judgment of 30 June 2009, ECLI:DE:BVerfG:2009:es20090630.2bve000208, para. 319, 414.

[66]Czech Constitutional Court, Pl. US 19/08, *Treaty of Lisbon I*, decision of 26 November 2008, ECLI:CZ:US:2008:Pl.US.19.08.1, para. 165–166.

opinions vis-à-vis their government or Head of State. In some Member States, a middle ground between previous consent/legally binding mandate on the one side and non-binding own initiative opinion of the parliament on the other is sought in the parliamentary scrutiny of draft EU legal acts and/or of the national executive's positions for Council and European Council meetings. For example, it may be prescribed that the government has to consult the matter with the Parliament if the Parliament so requires,[67] take the parliamentary position into account,[68] or that the opinion of the Parliament shall form the basis of the government's position.[69] It is not uncommon that this form of parliamentary participation is delegated to EU affairs committees in the Parliaments. The government is usually allowed to deviate from the parliamentary mandate, but only for qualified reasons specified by the law[70] and under the condition that the deviation is subsequently explained to the Parliament.[71] Where the Member State is represented in the European Council by the Head of Government, not following the parliamentary opinion runs into the risk of political consequences, in the extreme case even a vote of no confidence. This merely *political* mandate may in practice be understood in the national constitutional system as a very strong limit imposed upon the government (e.g. Finland, Sweden).[72] On the other hand, in political constellations where the government dominates the parliament, it may be a dead letter. Again, it needs to be stressed that the parliamentary scrutiny of the European Council and its political impact on the representative of the Member State is to a large extent a matter of political and constitutional practice in the respective Member State.[73]

---

[67]Of the Member States that have no special previous consent procedure related to Article 48(7) TEU, we can mention for example **Bulgaria** (Article 121 and 126 of the Rules of Procedure of the National Assembly), **Greece** (Article 32A(9) of the Standing Orders of the Parliament—stressing the merely consultative nature of these deliberations), **Finland** (Article 96 of the Constitution) or **Sweden** (Chapter 7, Article 14 and other provisions of the Riksdag Act).

[68]For example **Italy** (Article 7 of the Law No. 234/2012 of 24 December 2012 on general rules on Italy's participation in formation and implementation of EU legislation and policies); **Lithuania** (Article 3 of the Constitutional Act on Membership of the Republic of Lithuania in the European Union), **Romania** (Article 3 of the Act No. 373/2013 on cooperation between the Parliament and the Government in the field of European affairs), **Slovenia** (Article 10 of the Act on Cooperation between the National Assembly and the Government in EU affairs).

[69]For example **Croatia** (Article 8 of the Act on the Co-Operation of the Croatian Parliament and the Government of the Republic of Croatia in European Affairs), **Hungary** (Article 65 of the Act XXXVI of 2012 on the National Assembly).

[70]For example in **Hungary**: "in justified cases only" (Article 65 of Act XXXVI/2012 on the National Assembly); in **Slovakia**: "only in an unavoidable instance and with due consideration for the interest of the Slovak Republic" (Article 2(5) of the Constitutional Law on cooperation between the National Council of the Slovak Republic and the Government of the Slovak Republic in the affairs concerning the European Union).

[71]Including the possible vote on the acceptance of the justification (Article 67(2) of Act XXXVI/2012 on the National Assembly).

[72]Cf. Hegeland (2007).

[73]This is especially relevant in the many Member States where there is no express regulation regarding the parliamentary scrutiny of the European Council (as opposed to the Council). Where,

With a view to the course of the procedure in Article 48(7) TEU, additional safeguards and requirements can only refer to a voting mandate for a member of the European Council by his or her national Parliament, i.e. an additional (national) decision *before* the European Council member casts his vote. Any requirement in national law of a *subsequent* parliamentary approval of the European Council decision (in the sense of a ratification), that is, national parliamentary consent *after* the European Council has taken its decision, would be irrelevant from the point of view of European law. Different from the simplified revision procedure under Article 48(6) TEU and the procedures under Articles 42(2) and 49 TEU and Articles 25, 218 (8), 223(1), 262 and 311 TFEU, the Treaties do not provide that the European Council decision shall enter into force only after it has been "approved by the Member States in accordance with their respective constitutional requirements".[74]

4.5.3 *National Procedures of Previous Parliamentary Consent*

National procedures of previous parliamentary consent for the application of the general bridging clauses under Article 48(7) TEU have been adopted in eight Member States. In some cases, they do not only apply to the general bridging clauses of Article 48(7) TEU, but also to some or all of the special bridging clauses (see Sect. 4.6 below). Many of the rules regarding the previous consent are modelled after the procedure for ratification of international treaties in the respective Member States.

The **German** legislator implemented the Constitutional Court's aforementioned judgment with the Responsibility for Integration Act of 2009.[75] According to Section 4(1) of the Act, the German representative in the European Council may approve a proposal for a decision within the meaning of Article 48(7) of the TEU or abstain from voting on such a proposal only after a law to that effect as defined in Article 23(1) of the Basic Law has entered into force. The law under Article 23(1) requires a majority of two thirds of the Members of the Bundestag and two thirds of the votes of the Bundesrat (Article 79(2) of the Basic Law). If any such law leads to amendments to the Basic Law affecting the division of the Federation into *Länder*, their participation on principle in the legislative process, or the principles laid down in Articles 1 and 20, it shall be inadmissible (Article 79(3) of the Basic Law). In the

on the other hand, the national rules on parliamentary scrutiny in EU affairs refer to the scrutiny of draft legal acts, the rare instances when the European Council adopts legal acts should be covered by those rules.

[74] Cf. Craig (2011), p. 1894 f.

[75] Act on the Exercise by the Bundestag and by the Bundesrat of their Responsibility for Integration in Matters concerning the European Union (Responsibility for Integration Act) of 22 September 2009, as amended by Article 1 of the Act of 1 December 2009.

absence of a law under Article 23(1), the German representative in the European Council must reject the proposal for a decision.

In a similar fashion, the positive vote of the **Austrian** representative in the European Council is also dependent on a vote of approval by the Austrian parliament. Different from German law, the provision is contained directly in the Constitution and not in statutory law. According to Article 23i(1) of the Federal Constitutional Law the Austrian member in the European Council may agree to an initiative pursuant to Article 48(7) TEU only after having been authorized by the National Council (*Nationalrat*), with the consent of the Federal Council (*Bundesrat*), on the basis of a proposal of the Federal Government. Such resolutions of the National Council and the Federal Council each require the presence of at least half the members and a majority of two thirds of the votes cast.[76] The quora are the same as for state treaties modifying the Treaty basis of the European Union (Article 50(1) No. 2 of the Federal Constitutional Law). One major difference to the German situation is interesting to note: Article 23i(1) of the Federal Constitutional Law only covers the positive vote (consent) of the European Council representative. According to the wording of the provision, it is not excluded that the European Council representative, in the absence of a parliamentary mandate, simply abstains from a vote, which does not prevent the adoption of the European Council decision.[77] Such an interpretation significantly affects the power of that provision and offsets the high quorum for the adoption of the parliamentary act.

Likewise, **Ireland** has reacted with a constitutional amendment to the entry into force of the Treaty of Lisbon and the introduction of the general bridging clauses.[78] Article 29.4.8 of the Irish Constitution (*Bunreacht*) provides that the State (i.e. the government representative in the European Council) may agree to the decisions authorising the Council to act other than by unanimity or decisions authorising the adoption of the ordinary legislative procedure, but the agreement to any such decision shall be subject to the prior approval of both Houses of Parliament (the *Oireachtas*). The mandating system provided by the Constitution is not reflected in the Standing Orders of both Houses and thus the *Dáil* and the *Seanad* individually have to empower the government to agree to the initiative.[79] Therefore, the mandating system differs from the ordinary enactment of an act of parliament, which grants the *Seanad* only a suspensive veto. The changed role in the mandating system of Article 29.4.8 of the Constitution reflects the position of the Irish Senate for important decisions.[80]

The **United Kingdom** has also introduced a system of legally binding mandates for decisions on the passerelle clauses. According to Section 7, subsection 3, in

[76]See also Schmalenbach, in Mayer and Stöger (2013), Artikel 31 EUV, para. 27; Galiciani (2011), p. 182 f.

[77]With this remark Öhlinger and Potacs (2014), p. 26 f.

[78]Cf. Barrett (2013), p. 200 ff.

[79]See in more detail Barrett (2013), p. 200 ff.

[80]Cf. on this also Braune (2010), p. 442 f.

conjunction with subsection 4(b) of the European Union Act 2011, a Minister of the Crown may not vote in favour of or otherwise support a decision under Article 48 (7) of the TEU unless the draft decision is approved by Act of Parliament. In most of the cases, in which the bridging clauses can be activated, Section 6, subsection 1, in conjunction with subsection 5(b) of the European Union Act 2011 (in combination with Schedule 1 to the Act), a previous referendum is also required.[81] For legislative acts, the upper chamber, the *House of Lords*, disposes of a veto. However, this is only a suspensive veto which, under certain conditions, can be overruled by the *House of Commons*.[82]

In **Malta**, the use of the bridging clauses is not expressly covered by provisions of domestic law. Nonetheless, it is covered by more general provisions on parliamentary participation in European Union affairs. According to Article 2(2) of the European Union Act, the activation of the bridging clauses is treated as a treaty amendment, to which the Maltese representative in the European Council may not agree unless previously approved by the Maltese House of Representatives (*Kamra tad-Deputati*). The decision is taken by the plenary on the basis of a report from the Standing Committee on Foreign and European Affairs.[83]

In **Poland**, the National Assembly (*Zgromadzenie Narodowe*) is likewise empowered under domestic law to give instructions to the national European Council representative. On the basis of Article 14 of the Act of 8 October 2010 on the cooperation of the Council of Ministers with the Sejm and the Senate in matters relating to the Republic of Poland's membership of the European Union[84] a decision on Poland's position on a draft legal act referred to in Article 48(7) of the TEU, i.e. to support the adoption or to abstain, shall be taken by the President of the Republic of Poland on proposal of the Council of Ministers, with consent granted by statute. A draft statute is first adopted by the lower chamber, the *Sejm*, and then transferred to the Senate. The statute is passed if the Senate agrees or does not reply within thirty day. A rejection or amendment by the Senate can be overwritten by the *Sejm* with absolute majority. The draft must be signed by the Polish President in order to enter into force. If no statute is passed, the Polish representative in the European Council shall support the rejection of the draft legal act. This is in line with the Polish Constitutional Tribunal's view that EU decision-making creates obligations for the State and thus the national Parliament should be able to influence these rules through its government.[85]

---

[81]See alo Denza, in Blanke and Mangiameli (2013), Article 48 TEU, para. 51; Casalena, in Blanke and Mangiameli (2013), Protocol No. 1, para. 96 (on Article 6 of the Protocol); Craig (2011), p. 1894 f.

[82]Gebauer (2010), p. 418 f.

[83]Pace (2015), p. 583.

[84]The "Council of Ministers" is Poland's highest administrative body and commonly referred to as "the cabinet" (the government) and should not be confused with the "Council of Ministers" of the European Union.

[85]Polish Constitutional Tribunal, Ref. No. K 24/04, *Sejm/Senate in the EU Legislative Process*, judgment of 12 January 2005.

In **Denmark**, according to Section 1(2) of Act No. 321 from 30 April 2008 on the Ratification of the Lisbon Treaty, the Danish Government cannot sign up to a decision adopted by the European Council to activate a bridging clause under Article 48(7) of the TEU without the consent of the Danish *Folketing*. Consent is granted by an ordinary parliamentary decision by simple majority while more than half of the Members shall be present and take part in the voting.[86] If the specific use of the passerelle clause is considered as ceding sovereignty to international authorities, the parliamentary decision requires the consent of five sixths of the members of the *Folketing*. If the quorum is not met, the bill can only be adopted if accepted through referendum by a majority of voters and participation of at least 30% of all persons entitled to vote.[87]

The mandating system in the **Czech Republic** is laid down in the Rules of Procedure of the two parliamentary chambers. The Czech representative in the European Council must seek approval by both parliamentary chambers to support the activation of the bridging clause. The government's proposal that the chambers express the previous consent is first debated in the Committee on EU Affairs and then in the plenary. In the Chamber of Deputies the previous consent must be put to a vote within the six-month period prescribed by EU law. In the Senate, there is no such rule.[88] No qualified majority is prescribed for the granting of the consent, so, according to the general rule, a simple majority in the presence of at least one third of members of the chamber is sufficient. The possibility to adopt a resolution expressly opposing the initiative and the non-existent rules on cooperation of both chambers has already been mentioned.

4.5.4 European Council Voting Without National Parliamentary Consent

The problem that the possibility of "constructive abstention" of the national representative in the European Council is not covered by the wording of some of the aforementioned rules (Austria, Denmark, the Czech Republic, Ireland, Malta) can be resolved by interpretation. The purpose of the rules is clearly to ensure that the European Council decision is not adopted without the consent of the parliament concerned, which means that the Parliament remains in power to agree e.g. to the loss of the veto position of the Member State in the Council. This should mean that the representative in the European Council is not only prohibited from actively consenting

---

[86]Article 50 of the Constitutional Act of Denmark as well as Section 33 of the Standing Orders of the Danish Parliament.

[87]Article 20 of the Constitutional Act.

[88]Sections 109j (especially paragraph 7) and 109k in connection with Section 109i(c) of the Rules of Procedure of the Chamber of Deputies, Sections 119m and 119n of the Standing Rules of the Senate.

to the adoption of the decision but also from any tacit conduct that would have the same effect as the explicit consent. The other possible interpretation would make the whole procedure worthless and devoid of any meaning because an abstention from voting does not alter the legal obligations of the Member State arising from the adopted decision in any way. The national representative could easily circumvent the binding decision of the national Parliament. Hence we do not consider this to be a convincing interpretation. While from the perspective of EU law, it may be argued that there is the EU-law based veto power that should have been exercised by the parliament, the representative in the European Council is simultaneously bound by the national law regulating the previous consent. And, as explained above, the previous consent procedures are just a specific method of representative democracy, on which the Union is founded (Article 10 TEU), *within* the Member States. A "constructive abstention" of the national European Council representative who did not obtain the nationally prescribed previous consent of the Parliament would therefore violate national law.

If we look at these domestic procedures that require the national representative in the European Council to seek consent by Parliament prior to voting on the draft decision activating a bridging clause, one may wonder what happens if the national representative casts a vote supporting the draft decision (or abstains from voting, respectively), without or even against a decision by his or her national Parliament. In other words, what happens at the international (European) level, if a legal conflict arises in the national context (which, first and foremost has to be resolved at the national level)? While frankly, this situation is politically improbable, from a legal point of view it is not impossible. We shall therefore take a look at the relevance for and impact on the decision making at European level.

A similar situation is envisaged by Article 46(1) of the Vienna Convention on the Law of Treaties (1969),[89] according to which a State may not invoke the fact that its consent to be bound by a treaty has been expressed in violation of a provision of its internal law regarding competence to conclude treaties as invalidating its consent unless that violation was manifest and concerned a rule of its internal law of fundamental importance. This provision is a narrow exception to the rule of Article 27 of the Convention that a party may not invoke the provisions of its internal law as justification for its failure to perform a treaty.[90] A rule of fundamental importance is any provision of the (substantive) constitutional law with importance for the institutional and political structure of the State and for the relationship between State and citizens.[91] This idea may be applied also to the European law question at stake. Since a domestic mandating system exceeds the European law requirements of Article 48 (7) TEU, it is *prima facie* without relevance to the adopting of the decision to

[89]It is held that this provision (today) is declaratory of customary international law. See Villiger (2009), Article 46, para. 19; Jennings and Watts (1992), para. 636.

[90]Cf. Rensmann, in Dörr and Schmalenbach (2012), Article 46, para. 22.

[91]Rensmann, in Dörr and Schmalenbach (2012), Article 46, para. 39. According to Villiger (2009), Article 46. para. 16, a rule is of fundamental importance only "if it directly relates to, and provides an essential condition for, the competence to conclude a treaty". This definition, however, is too restrictive to take account of the intention of Article 46 of the Convention.

activate the bridging clause unless it is of fundamental importance in domestic law. As seen in Germany, the requirement for a mandate for the European Council representative was introduced in order to compensate for the lack of the requirement to ratify this type of Treaty amendment. As such, according to national (constitutional) law, the mandating requirement is of fundamental importance; from the point of view of European law it is part of the fundamental political and constitutional structures and thus an expression of the national identity of a Member States that the European Union is obliged to respect (Article 4(2) TEU).

However, under Article 46 of the Vienna Convention, the violation of the internal rule must also be "manifest". According to paragraph 2 of Article 46, a violation is manifest if it would be objectively evident to any State conducting itself in the matter in accordance with normal practice and in good faith. This is the case if another State had actual knowledge of the violation or if it ought to have known (negligent ignorance).[92] On the basis of Article 7 of the Convention, it is presumed that Head of State or Heads of Government have full powers to represent their State. Other States therefore cannot be expected to question this authority. Hence, as a general rule, a violation can only be considered manifest if it was easily ascertainable and could have been established by any other State without further investigation as a matter of common knowledge.[93] Against this background, there is now clear-cut answer as to whether the lack of a mandate would be easily ascertainable to the other European Council members. Since Article 48(7) TEU provides only that the national Parliaments have the right to veto an initiative under that provision, the lack of a parliamentary veto supports the assumption that no further obstacles exist for taking the decision. As a result, a positive vote (or abstention) of a European Council member without or against a national parliamentary authorisation does not hinder the entry into force of a decision to activate a bridging clause. Therefore it may be practical, in case of denial of previous consent to the national representative in the European Council, to simultaneously make known the opposition of the parliament to the initiative according to Article 48(7) TEU—provided, of course, that the conditions for casting a valid veto have been met by the national Parliament.

[92]Rensmann, in Dörr and Schmalenbach (2012), Article 46, para. 45.

[93]Rensmann, in Dörr and Schmalenbach (2012), Article 46, para. 48; Villiger (2009), Article 46, para. 12, both with further references.

4.6 Relevance of the Interpretation of the Procedure for Activating the General Bridging Clauses for the Special Bridging Clauses

It is worth mentioning that many of the conclusions reached above regarding the procedural aspects of the general bridging clauses are also *mutatis mutandis* relevant for the corresponding rules applicable to the special bridging clauses.

The interpretation of EU law rules on the veto power under Article 48(7) TEU is also relevant to the veto power under the third subparagraph of Article 81(3) TFEU. On the other hand, the European Parliament is merely consulted under the second subparagraph of Article 81(3) TFEU.

In some Member States, national law regulates the exercise of the veto power under the third subparagraph of Article 81(3) TFEU in a way that is materially identical to the rules discussed above regarding the exercise of the veto power under Article 48(7) TEU.[94] This makes the conclusions in Sect. 4.3 also relevant for these cases.

Finally, in some Member States, national law regulates the prior consent of the parliament not only in relation to the adoption of the European Council decision under Article 48(7) TEU, but also in relation to some or all the special bridging clauses.[95] This makes the conclusions in Sect. 4.5 also relevant for these cases.

---

[94] **Austria**: Article 23i(2) of the Federal Constitutional Law; **Czech Republic**: Section 109j (especially paragraph 7) and 109k in connection with Section 109i of the Rules of Procedure of the Chamber of Deputies, Section 119m and 119n of the Standing Rules of the Senate; **France**: Article 88-7 of the Constitution; **Germany**: Section 4(2) of the Act on the Exercise by the Bundestag and by the Bundesrat of their Responsibility for Integration in Matters concerning the European Union; **Ireland**: Article 7(2) of the European Union Act 2009; **Italy**: Article 11(5) of the Law No. 234/2012 of 24 December 2012 on general rules on Italy's participation in formation and implementation of EU legislation and policies; **Poland**: Article 148cb of the Standing Orders of the Sejm and Article 75f and 75g of the Rules and Regulations of the Senat; **Slovenia**: Section 154p of the of the Rules of Procedure of the National Assembly (as opposed to the veto under the general bridging clause, the Rules of Procedure allow the final decision to be made by a committee, unless the committee or one quarter of the deputies request that the matter be decided by the plenary); **Spain**: Article 3(n) in connection with Article 8 of the Law 8/1994 regulating the Joint Parliamentary European Union Committee (as amended by Law 24/2009) in connection with Article 10 of the Resolution of the Bureaus of the Congress of Deputies and the Senate of 21 September 1995 developing Law of 21 September 1995 (as amended by Resolution of 27 May 2010). Further national rules expressly related to the special bridging clause of Article 81(3) TFEU only deal with the organisation of the procedure in the parliament.

[95] **Czech Republic**: prior consent of both chambers of Parliament (Section 109l of the Rules of Procedure of the Chamber of Deputies; Section 119k and 119m of the Standing Rules of the Senate); **Denmark**: prior consent of the Parliament applicable in general to all bridging clauses (Section 1(2) of Act No. 321 from 30 April 2008 on the Ratification of the Lisbon Treaty); **Germany**: prior consent of the German Bundestag and, should the decision touch upon areas related to the competence of the *Länder*, also of the Federal Council, applicable to all the special bridging clauses without veto as listed in Section 5 and 6 of the Act on the Exercise by the Bundestag and by the Bundesrat of their Responsibility for Integration in Matters concerning the European Union; **Ireland**: prior consent of both chambers of the Parliament applicable in general to all bridging clauses (Article 29(8) of the Constitution); **Poland**: prior consent in the form of an

References

Barrett G (2013) The Oireachtas and the European Union. Houses of the Oireachtas, Dublin

Barrett G (2015) Long train running: the slowly developed (and slowly developing) role of Ireland's oireachtas in EU affairs. In: Hefftler C, Neuhold C, Rozenberg O, Smith J (eds) The Palgrave handbook of national parliaments and the European Union. Palgrave, Basingstoke, pp 290–311

Besselink LFM, Mourik B (2012) The parliamentary legitimacy of the European Union: the role of the states general within the European Union. Utrecht Law Rev 28–50

Blanke H-J, Mangiameli S (eds) (2013) The treaty on European Union—a commentary. Springer, Heidelberg

Blanke H-J, Böttner R (2015) The democratic deficit in the economic governance of the European Union. In: Blanke H-J, Cruz Villalón P, Klein T, Ziller J (eds) Common European legal thinking. Essays in honour of Albrecht Weber. Springer, Heidelberg, pp 243–286

Böttner R (2016) The treaty amendment procedures and the relationship between Article 31(3) TEU and the general bridging clause of Article 48(7) TEU. Eur Const Law Rev 499–521

Braune F (2010) Seanad Éireann – Die Zweite Kammer Irlands. In Riescher G, Ruß S, Haas CM (eds) Zweite Kammern, 2nd edn. Oldenbourg Verlag, Munich, pp 433–450

Burgorgue-Larsen L, Levade A, Picod F (eds) (2007) Traité établissant une Constitution pour l'Europe, Partie I et IV. Bruylant, Brussels

Calliess C, Ruffert M (eds) (2016) EUV/AEUV, 5th edn. C.H. Beck, Munich

Costato L, Rossi LS, Borghi P (eds) (2015) Commentario alla Legge 24.12.2012 n. 234. Editoriale Scientifica, Naples

Craig P (2011) The European Union Act 2011: locks, limits and legality. Common Mark Law Rev 1915–1944

Delreux T, Randour F (2015) Belgium: institutional and administrative adaptation but limited political interest. In: Hefftler C, Neuhold C, Rozenberg O, Smith J (eds) The Palgrave handbook of national parliaments and the European Union. Palgrave, Basingstoke, pp 153–169

Deschouwer K (2012) The politics of Belgium, 2nd edn. Palgrave, Basingstoke

Dörr O, Schmalenbach K (eds) (2012) Vienna convention on the law of treaties. Springer, Heidelberg

Elgie R (ed) (1999) Semi-presidentialism in Europe. OUP, Oxford

Esposito A (2013) La Legge 24 dicembre 2012, n. 234, sulla partecipazione dell'Italia alla formazione e all'attuazione della normativa e delle politiche dell'Unione Europea. federalismi. it 2/2013

European Parliament (2013) Democratic control in the member states of the European council and the euro zone summits. Study. PE 474.392. European Parliament, Brussels. Available at: http://www.europarl.europa.eu/thinktank/en/document.html?reference=IPOL-AFCO_ET%282013%29474392

Gabanyi AU (2010) Das politische System Rumäniens. In: Ismayr W (ed) Die politischen Systeme Osteuropas, 3rd edn. VS, Wiesbaden, pp 627–676

Galiciani B (2011) Die Stärkung der Mitwirkungsrechte des Nationalrates und Bundesrates durch die Lissabon-Begleitnovelle. J für Rechtspolitik 173–183

Gamper A (2011) Zweite Kammern und ihre Europaarbeit nach Lissabon. In: Abels G, Eppler A (eds) Auf dem Weg zum Mehrebenenparlamentarismus? Funktionen von Parlamenten im politischen System der EU. Nomos, Baden Baden, pp 243–260

act, applicable to all the special bridging clauses as listed in Section 14 and 15 of the Act of 8 October 2010 on the cooperation of the Council of Ministers with the Sejm and the Senate in matters relating to the Republic of Poland's membership of the European Union; **United Kingdom**: prior consent in the form of an act or by a referendum applicable to all the special bridging clauses as listed in Section 5 of the European Union Act 2011.

Gebauer B (2010) Das britische Oberhaus: Auf dem Weg zu mehr Demokratie? In: Riescher G, Ruß S, Haas CM (eds) Zweite Kammern, 2nd edn. Oldenbourg Verlag, Munich, pp 407–432
Grabitz E, Hilf M, Nettesheim M (eds) (2009 ff.) Das Recht der Europäischen Union: EUV/AEUV. Loose leaf. C.H.Beck, Munich
Granat K (2016) Interparliamentary cooperation and the simplified revision procedures. In: Lupo N, Fasone C (eds) Interparliamentary cooperation in the composite European constitution. Hart, Oxord, pp 73–90
Groß T (2003) Zwei-Kammer-Parlamente in der Europäischen Union. Zeitschrift für ausländisches öffentliches Recht und Völkerrecht, 29–57
Haas CM (2010) Sein oder nicht sein: Bikameralismus und die Funktion Zweiter Kammern. In: Riescher G, Ruß S, Haas CM (eds) Zweite Kammern, 2nd edn. Oldenbourg Verlag, Munich, pp 3–21
Hegeland H (2007) The European Union in national parliaments: domestic or foreign policy? A study of Nordic parliamentary systems. In: O'Brennan J, Raunio T (eds) National parliaments within the enlarged European Union. From 'victims' of integration to competitive actors? Routledge, London, New York, pp 95–115
Högenauer A-L (2015) The Dutch parliament and EU affairs: decentralizing scrutiny. In: Hefftler C, Neuhold C, Rozenberg O, Smith J (eds) The Palgrave handbook of national parliaments and the European Union. Palgrave, Basingstoke, pp 252–271
Ionescu C (2014) Romania. In: Besselink L et al (eds) Constitutional law of EU member states. Kluwer, Deventer, pp 1351–1425
Jennings RY, Watts A (1992) Oppenheim's international law, 9th edn. OUP, Oxford
Kempf U (2009) Das politische System Frankreichs. In: Ismayr W (ed) Die politischen Systeme Westeuropas, 4th edn. VS, Wiesbaden, pp 349–404
Kiiver P (2012) The early warning system for the principle of subsidiarity. Routledge, London
Kortmann C (2014) The French republic. In: Besselink L et al (eds) Constitutional law of EU member states. Kluwer, Deventer, pp 569–641
Markides A (2014) The Republic of Cyprus. In: Besselink L et al (eds) Constitutional law of EU member states. Kluwer, Deventer, pp 249–319
Mavčič AM (2014) The Republic of Slovenia. In: Besselink L et al (eds) Constitutional law of EU member states. Kluwer, Deventer, pp 1463–1519
Mayer M (2012) Die Europafunktion der nationalen Parlamente in der Europäischen Union. Mohr Siebeck, Tübingen
Mayer H, Stöger K (eds) (2013) Kommentar zu EUV und AEUV. Manz, Vienna
Niedobitek M (2011) Die Integrationsverantwortung von Bundestag und Bundesrat nach dem „Lissabon-Urteil" des Bundesverfassungsgerichts. In: Abels G, Eppler A (eds) Auf dem Weg zum Mehrebenenparlamentarismus? Funktionen von Parlamenten im politischen System der EU. Nomos, Baden Baden, pp 159–176
Öhlinger T, Potacs M (2014) EU-Recht und staatliches Recht, 5th edn. LexisNexis, Vienna
Pace R (2015) The Maltese Parliament and EU affairs: a slow awakening to its responsibilities. In: Hefftler C, Neuhold C, Rozenberg O, Smith J (eds) The Palgrave handbook of national parliaments and the European Union. Palgrave, Basingstoke, pp 578–593
Pechstein M, Nowak C, Häde U (eds) (2017) Frankfurter Kommentar zu EUV, GRC und AEUV. Mohr Siebeck, Tübingen
Peers, S. (2012). The future of EU treaty amendments. Yearb Eur Law 17–111
Popelier P, Lemmens K (2015) The constitution of Belgium. Hart, Oxford
Schüttemeyer S, Sturm R (1992) Wozu Zweite Kammern? Zur Repräsentation und Funktionalität Zweiter Kammern in westlichen Demokratien. Zeitschrift für Parlamentsfragen 517–536
Schwarz-Liebermann von Wahlendorf HA (1958) Struktur und Funktion der sogenannten Zweiten Kammer. Eine Studie zum Problem der Gewaltenteilung. Mohr, Tübingen
Swenden W, Brans M, De Winter L (2006) The politics of Belgium: institutions and policy under bipolar and centrifugal federalism. West Eur Polit 863–873
Tauber J (2010) Das politische System Litauens. In: Ismayr W (ed) Die politischen Systeme Osteuropas, 3rd edn. VS, Wiesbaden, pp 171–208

Vaičaitis VA (2014) The Republic of Lithuania. In: Besselink L et al (eds) Constitutional law of EU member states. Kluwer, Deventer, pp 1025–1083
Vehar P (2007) The national assembly of the Republic of Slovenia and EU affairs before and after accession. In: O'Brennan J, Raunio T (eds) National parliaments within the enlarged European Union. From 'victims' of integration to competitive actors? Routledge, London, New York, pp 241–254
Villiger ME (2009) Commentary on the 1969 Vienna convention on the law of treaties. Brill/Nijhoff, Leiden
Vilpišauskas R (2015) Parliamentary scrutiny of EU affairs in Lithuania: The dog that rarely barks. In: Hefftler C, Neuhold C, Rozenberg O, Smith J (eds) The Palgrave handbook of national parliaments and the European Union. Palgrave, Basingstoke, pp 563–569
Wendel M (2011) Permeabilität im europäischen Verfassungsrecht. Mohr Siebeck, Tübingen
Zervakis PA, Costeas T (2010) Die politischen Systeme Zyperns. In: Ismayr W (ed) Die politischen Systeme Osteuropas, 3rd edn. VS, Wiesbaden, pp 1097–1157

Chapter 5
Conclusions and Prospects

The Treaty of Lisbon has introduced a new supranational element in the logic of European integration by installing a simplified revision procedure in the form of the bridging clauses. With a procedure that is distinct from classic public international law, the founding treaties of the European Union can be amended without the need for formal ratification procedure in all Member States. The underlying purpose of the bridging clauses is to gradually accelerate the decision-making procedures and shift the "centre of gravity" from the Member States to the Commission and the European Parliament.

In ordert to prevent autonomous Treaty amendments by the Union and its institutions, Article 48(7) TEU grants any national Parliament the right to veto an amendment under this procedure. This right is rooted in European law, but may need implementation by domestic law in the individual Member States. This covers the procedures for casting the national parliamentary veto, including coordination between the two parliamentary chambers in bicameral system. In this respect, some Member States' domestic implementation is not in conformity with the requirements of European law.

For reasons of politics or constitutional law, some Member States' legal orders regard the granting of a parliamentary veto as insufficient to compensate for the loss of the requirement to ratify Treaty amendments. They therefore constructed procedures that make the voting of the national representative in the (European) Council depended on a decision by their national Parliaments. However, the binding effect is only in the domestic context between the parliament and the (European) Council member. It does not have any immediate legal effect on the European level, which may become relevant in the case of voting of a (European) Council member without or against a national parliamentary decision.

All in all, we can only draw a very heterogeneous picture of national reactions towards the introduction of the bridging clauses. Some Member States have introduced domestic procedures not only for the casting of the national Parliament's veto, but also for mandating the national representative at European level. The procedures in parts foresee high quora and even exceed the veto positions granted

R. Böttner and J. Grinc, *Bridging Clauses in European Constitutional Law*,
SpringerBriefs in Law, https://doi.org/10.1007/978-3-319-73341-8_5

by European law. On the other hand, we find Member States that pay little or almost no attention to the bridging clauses. The strength of parliamentary participation in these States therefore results only from the general constitutional logic and architecture. As a result, the application of the passerelle clauses is dependent on numerous hurdles and restrictions. Thus, it is difficult to speak of a truly "simplified" revision procedure. It is also apparent that although Article 48(7) TEU attempted to regulate directly the participation of the national Parliaments in this form of simplified Treaty amendment, its rules find manifold counterparts in various Member States, so that we cannot speak of a unified procedure.

It does not come as a surprise then that, to this day, the bridging clauses have not been applied in practice and the question may be asked whether they will ever be used. The most obvious obstacle is the necessity to reach a unanimous decision among the Member States. The Commission discouraged the Member States from upholding the unanimity requirement in the bridging clause already during the 2003–2004 Intergovernmental Conference, noting that "[t]he draft Constitution gives the European Council the option of deciding that an area in which the Council takes decisions on a unanimous basis will henceforth come under the rules for qualified majority voting (Article I-24(4)). But this 'passerelle' also requires a unanimous decision from the European Council and experience has shown that the general arrangements of this type introduced by the Maastricht and Amsterdam Treaties have never been used."[1]

Passing to qualified majority voting means giving up the veto power of each individual Member State. It is in the most politically salient areas of conferred competences where the Member States decided to retain the veto power of each one of them and at least some might not want to change this. Should the use of a bridging clause be proposed, a Member State would likely form its position based on whether its policy priorities in the policy area in question are best achieved under unanimous or majority decision-making. Possible future developments of EU policies are subject to almost continuous debates in the Council and its specialised preparatory bodies during legislative sessions and in reaction to various non-legislative prospective documents published by the Commission. Therefore, it may even be assumed that it would be clear to the Member States to what end the activation of a bridging clause is proposed, i.e. the adoption of which concrete measures that do not have unanimous support it should facilitate. A Member State would logically have to vote against the use of the bridging clause, if it did not wish to extend EU legislation in certain policy areas or change the status quo or was worried that it would find itself in a minority position and that its political preferences would not be carried to the legal act adopted by qualified majority to the extent that they would have had to be taken into account under unanimity rule.

[1]Communication from the Commission, A Constitution for the Union. Opinion of the Commission, pursuant to Article 48 of the Treaty on European Union, on the Conference of representatives of the Member States' governments convened to revise the Treaties, COM (2003) 548 final, at p. 5.

Available online http://www.cvce.eu/obj/communication_from_the_commission_a_constitution_for_the_union_17_september_2003-en-6058189d-d402-4d4d-a684-a0d2c56cc876.html.

Hence, bridging clauses can only be used if consensus is reached that a subject matter shall henceforth be subject to qualified majority voting or the ordinary legislative procedure. While technically possible to be applied to individual legislative initiatives, bridging clauses are not designed to overcome individual blocking positions for a certain dossier. For these instances, the instrument of enhanced cooperation is the practical way to go.[2]

The requirement of unanimity seems to be a hurdle that can hardly be overcome. However, the political reality often offers more complex situations which may make the triggering of the bridging clause more likely. Certainly, it has been possible for the Member States from the beginning of the European integration project to relinquish their veto power. The progressive introduction of qualified majority voting and co-decision was facilitated mainly by the fact that treaty reforms are big package deals amending or newly introducing multiple provisions in the Treaties. Also of importance was the growing number and heterogeneity of the Member States (especially between the Treaty of Nice and the Treaty of Lisbon) and various opt-outs agreed during the treaty reforms.

It is perhaps theoretically possible to have such smaller package deals on the level of secondary law. A Member State may for example give its consent with the use of a bridging clause related to a certain policy in exchange for an opt-out from (parts) of such policy or for concessions in a different policy area.

Another possible incentive for introducing qualified majority voting can arise from the complex system of EU law itself. As new legal acts are introduced under legal bases requiring unanimous decision-making, the problem arises with the rigid procedure of their subsequent amendment. In a theoretical situation, a majority of the Member States could prefer to amend the legal act in question, yet they would be stopped by a small minority holding on to their preferred status quo. In order to avoid such problems, the Member States may resort to empowering the Commission to adopt delegated or implementing acts (Articles 290 and 291 TFEU). But this may not be the preferred solution in politically salient issues due to the perceived insufficiency of Member States' control over the exercise of these powers by the Commission.[3] The other possibility would be to trigger the bridging clause in order to enable more flexible revisions of the legal act in question. Here, it must be added that the policy of the Commission to conjure a qualified-majority voting legal basis for almost any controversial piece of legislation[4] does mitigate this problem to a great extent and may be one of the important practical reasons why the bridging clauses have not yet been activated.

As opposed to the consensus of the Member States, the requirement in Article 48(7) TEU that the European Council shall act after obtaining the consent of the European Parliament, which shall be given by a majority of its component

---

[2]Cf. Böttner (2016).

[3]Of course according to Article 291(2) TFEU the power to adopt implementing acts may also be entrusted to the Council itself.

[4]See Schütze (2013), pp. 133–151; Weatherill (2011).

members, constitutes no real obstacle in the procedure from the political point of view. Any amendment of the decision-making procedures possible under this bridging clause strengthens the position of the European Parliament vis-à-vis the Member States (even the mere passing to qualified majority voting in the Council, which makes it easier for the Council to adopt its position and accommodate the position of the European Parliament). It seems natural that the European Parliament would be ready to support any such initiative.

The European Parliament has recently called for making an extensive use of the bridging clauses as a means for improving the functioning of the European Union building on the potential of the Lisbon Treaty. In its own initiative resolution, it called on the European Council "to make use of the 'passerelle clause' (Article 48(7) TEU) authorising the Council to switch from unanimity to QMV in applicable cases where the Treaties currently require unanimity",[5] advocated "the general use of the 'passerelle clause' enshrined in Article 48(7) TEU",[6] called "for the use of Article 31(2) TEU, which allows the Council to take certain decisions on CFSP matters by QMV, and the 'passerelle clause' contained in Article 31(3) TEU to switch progressively to QMV for decisions in the area of the CFSP that do not have military or defence implications",[7] and found it imperative "to strengthen the role of Parliament as co-legislator, on an equal footing with the Council, through the use of Article 81(3) TFEU, which makes it possible to switch decision-making in the field of family law with cross-border implications to the ordinary legislative procedure if the Council decides so unanimously, after having consulted Parliament; calls for a switch in decision-making on all other policies in the field of JHA to the ordinary legislative procedure, using the 'passerelle clause' in Article 48(7) TEU."[8] This would amount to almost a total exhaustion of the amending possibilities provided by the bridging clauses.

However, it is clear that the European Parliament is aware of the low probability that such a giant leap in the decision-making procedures will be made. In its resolution on possible evolutions of and adjustments to the current institutional set-up of the European Union, it notes that "none of the 'passerelle clauses' provided for in the Lisbon Treaty with a view to streamlining the Union's governance have been deployed, and are unlikely to be so in the present circumstances".[9]

A certain possibility for the European Parliament to press its claims could lie in forcing the Member States to trade off an extension of Parliament's co-decision powers via the use of a bridging clause for obtaining the Parliament's consent with a decision important for the Member States. The European Parliament has indeed already indicated such a consideration in relation to enhanced cooperation when it

---

[5]European Parliament resolution of 16 February 2017 on improving the functioning of the European Union building on the potential of the Lisbon Treaty (2014/2249(INI)), para. 27.

[6]European Parliament resolution 2014/2249(INI), para. 79.

[7]European Parliament resolution 2014/2249(INI), para. 102.

[8]European Parliament resolution 2014/2249(INI), para. 135.

[9]European Parliament resolution 2014/2249(INI), preambular paragraph AA.

stated that it "[i]s determined to implement fully the Treaty provisions on enhanced cooperation by committing not to give its consent to any new enhanced cooperation proposals unless the participating Member States commit to activate the special 'passerelle clause' enshrined in Article 333 TFEU to switch from unanimity to QMV, and from a special to the ordinary legislative procedure".[10] Yet the European Parliament did not proceed accordingly when it consented to the establishment of the European Public Prosecutor's Office,[11] although there is no indication that the Council intends to activate the special bridging clause of Article 333 TFEU regarding this regulation. Interestingly, the European Parliament had called on the Council to activate this special bridging clause already in 2010 when consenting to the first enhanced cooperation.[12]

Most recently, the President of the European Commission, *Jean-Claude Juncker*, hinted at the possible use of the bridging clauses in his 2017 State of the European Union speech.[13] He stated: "When it comes to important single market questions, I want decisions in the Council to be taken more often and more easily by qualified majority—with the equal involvement of the European Parliament. We do not need to change the Treaties for this. There are so-called 'passerelle clauses' in the current Treaties which allow us to move from unanimity to qualified majority voting in certain areas—if all Heads of State or Government agree to do so. I am also strongly in favour of moving to qualified majority voting for decisions on the common consolidated corporate tax base, on VAT, on fair taxes for the digital industry and on the financial transaction tax. Europe has to be able to act quicker and more decisively… I want our Union to become a stronger global actor. In order to have more weight in the world, we must be able to take foreign policy decisions quicker. This is why I want Member States to look at which foreign policy decisions could be moved from unanimity to qualified majority voting. The Treaty already provides for this, if all Member States agree to do it." This is remarkable because in the area of single market, unanimous decision-making by the Member States or a limited involvement of the European Parliament is generally encountered only very rarely.[14] The notable exception is found in the area of taxation, where the EU may run into the abovementioned problem of having a complex regulatory framework in need of frequent adjustments, which would require either many broad delegations of powers to the Commission or unanimous agreement of the Member States on any amendment.

---

[10] European Parliament resolution 2014/2249(INI), para. 23.

[11] European Parliament legislative resolution of 5 October 2017 on the draft Council regulation implementing enhanced cooperation on the establishment of the European Public Prosecutor's Office ("the EPPO") (2013/0255/APP).

[12] European Parliament legislative resolution of 16 June 2010 on the draft Council decision authorising enhanced cooperation in the area of the law applicable to divorce and legal separation (2010/0066(NLE)), point 2.

[13] http://europa.eu/rapid/press-release_SPEECH-17-3165_en.htm.

[14] Cf. Article 114 TFEU, which in the practice of the Commission often takes precedence over more specific legal bases.

The 2018 Commission work programme confirms that the Commission will "outline how the EU could make use of the so-called 'passerelle clauses' in the current Treaties which allow us to move from unanimity to qualified majority voting in certain areas if all Heads of State or Government agree to do so. We will do this for internal market matters, as well as for certain foreign policy decisions to ensure the Union is a strong global actor with real weight in the world, while paying particular attention to the consistency and efficiency of these decisions." A detailed Communication from the Commission can be expected in the third quarter of 2018.[15]

Whether the abovementioned possibilities materialise in practice is yet to be seen. The current political climate in the EU makes any kind of revision of the Treaties unlikely to accommodate everybody and succeed, which, as the European Parliament notes, should lead us to exploiting possibilities of the current treaty framework. However, in this respect the bridging clauses do not really help much, because they do not permit any material changes to EU competence and still require unanimity of the Member States.

References

Böttner R (2016) Eine Idee lernt laufen – zur Praxis der Verstärkten Zusammenarbeit nach Lissabon. Zeitschrift für europarechtliche Studien, 501–549

Schütze R (2013) From dual to cooperative federalism. The changing structure of European law. Oxford University Press, Oxford

Weatherill S (2011) The limits of legislative harmonization ten years after tobacco advertising: how the court's case law has become a 'drafting guide'. Ger Law J 12(3):827–864

[15]Communication from the Commission, Commission Work Programme 2018—An agenda for a more united, stronger and more democratic Europe, COM(2017) 650 of 24 October 2017, pp. 11–12 and No. 26 in Annex 1.f.

FSC
www.fsc.org
MIX
Papier | Fördert
gute Waldnutzung
FSC® C083411

Kolibri 360 GmbH
Ferdinand-Jühlke-Straße 7
99095 Erfurt, Deutschland
produktsicherheit@kolibri360.de